POSTCARDS 4

SECOND EDITION

Brian Abbs • Chris Barker • Ingrid Freebairn
with JJ Wilson *and* Stella Reilly

PEARSON
Longman

Postcards 4, Second Edition

Authorized adaptation from the United Kingdom edition, entitled *Snapshot*, first edition, published by Pearson Education Limited publishing under its Longman imprint. Copyright © 1998.

American English adaptation, published by Pearson Education, Inc. Copyright © 2008.

Copyright © 2008 by Pearson Education, Inc. All rights reserved. No part of this publication may be reproduced, stored in a retrieval system, or transmitted in any form or by any means, electronic, mechanical, photocopying, recording, or otherwise, without the prior permission of the publisher.

Pearson Education, 10 Bank Street, White Plains, NY 10606

Staff credits: The people who made up the **Postcards 4, Second Edition** team, representing editorial, production, design, and manufacturing, are Aerin Csigay, Dave Dickey, Nancy Flaggman, Ann France, Charles Green, Mike Kemper, Ed Lamprich, Melissa Leyva, Sherri Pemberton, Liza Pleva, Nicole Santos, and Jane Townsend.
Cover and text design: Ann France
Text composition: TSI Graphics
Text font: 11/14 Palatino

ISBN-13: 978-0-13-243925-1
ISBN-10: 0-13-243925-5

2 3 4 5 6 7 8 9 10—QWD—12 11 10 09 08 07

Illustration credits
Steve Attoe: pp. 9, 27, 53, 75, 92; Mark Collins: pp. 22, 83, 94, 111; Tim Haggerty: 66; Mike Hortens: pp. 7, 17, 39, 100; Barbara Pollak: p. 10; Rodica Prato: p. 4; Chris Reed: p. 48; Bart Rivers: p. 67, 112, 113; Rob Schuster: pp. 50, 98–99; Matt Straub: p. 78; Anna Veltfort: pp. 38, 95, 106; William Waitzman: pp. 2, 5; Ron Zalme: p. 47.

Text credits
p. 47 Redwood Publishing for an adapted extract from "Smashing Stereotypes" by Gary Parkinson in *AA Members Magazine* 28.8.98; p.68 www.slothclub.org; p. 76 *TIME* magazine, December 31, 1999; p. 98 © 2002 TIME Inc. reprinted by permission.

Photo credits
All original photography by Michal Heron; cover (city) Jeremy Woodhouse/Getty Images, (globe) Erik Dreyer; borders (globe) Larry Williams/Corbis, (clouds) Royalty-Free/Corbis; p. 3 (1) Corbis/Jupiterimages, (2) DesignPics Inc./Index Stock Imagery, (3) Lourens Smak/Alamy, (4) Michael Keller/Corbis, (5) Ralf-Finn Hestoft/Index Stock Imagery, (6) Andrey Stratilatov/Shutterstock.com, (7) Royalty-Free/Corbis, (8) Charles Gupton/StockBoston; p. 6 Panoramic Images/Getty Images; p. 7 age fotostock/SuperStock; p. 11 (top left) Tony Stone Images, (top middle) Britstock-IFA, (top right) Royalty-Free/Corbis, (left) Telegraph Colour Library, (middle) Greg Evans International, (right) David L. Moore/Alamy, (bottom left) Telegraph Colour Library; p. 17 AP Images; p. 18 Henryk T. Kaiser/Index Stock Imagery; p. 20 (background) Charles O'Rear/Corbis, (top left) Robert Landau/Corbis, (top right) Animals Animals/Earth Scenes, (middle) Gary Ranell/Getty Images, (bottom left) Chad Ehlers/Getty Images; p. 23 Dave G. Houser/Corbis; p. 28 David Young-Wolff/Getty Images; p. 29 (top and bottom) Lisette Le Bon/SuperStock; p. 32 (background) David Pu'u/Corbis, (top) Bernice P. Bishop Museum, Honolulu; p. 33 (left) Bernice P. Bishop Museum, Honolulu, (bottom) Warren Bolster/Getty Images; p. 37 Royalty-Free/Corbis; p. 40 (1) SW Productions/Getty Images, (2) David Young-Wolff/PhotoEdit, (3) Jean du Boisberranger/Getty Images, (4) Harald Sund/Getty Images; p. 46 Raeanne Rubenstein/Index Stock Imagery; p. 47 (left to right) Kevin Peterson/Getty Images, Photodisc/Getty Images, Kevin Peterson/Getty Images, Amos Morgan/Getty Images; p. 48 FoodPix; p. 52 (left) Images.com/Corbis, (top right) David Young-Wolff/PhotoEdit, (right) Jay Koelzer/Index Stock Imagery, (middle) Gabe Palmer/Corbis, (bottom) Dorling Kindersley; p. 55 Lisa Henderling/Images.com; p. 56 (top) Bob Rowan/Progressive Image/Corbis, (middle) Robert Glusic/Getty Images, (bottom) Harry DiOrio/Syracuse Newspapers/The Image Works; p. 60 www.vivometrics.com; p. 61 (top right) Dragan Trifunovic/Shutterstock.com, (bottom) Jaimie Duplass/Shutterstock.com; p. 65 Lawson Wood; p. 68 (left) The Skyfish Project, (right) AP Images; p. 72 (left) Miramax/The Kobal Collection, (middle) 20th Century Fox/The Kobal Collection, (right) New Line/The Kobal Collection; p. 73 Frank Trapper/Corbis; p. 76 (left and right) Bettmann/Corbis; p. 79 (background) G.D.T./Getty Images, (top) Patrick Darby/Corbis, (bottom) Thom Lang/Corbis; p. 86 Ariel Skelley/Corbis; p. 88 (top) Jim McGuire/Index Stock Imagery, (bottom) Pallava Bagla/Corbis Sygma; p. 89 Danita Delimont/Alamy; p. 91 Ben Siegfried; p. 96 (left) Rick Doyle/Corbis, (right) Jim Sugar Photography/Corbis; p. 102 Bob Daemmrich/The Image Works; p. 103 (1) Kevin Galvin/age fotostock, (2) Royalty-Free/Corbis, (3) Gary Crabbe/age fotostock, (4) Jon Arnold/age fotostock, (5) Doug Scott/age fotostock, (6) Sergio Pitamitz/Corbis, (7) Royalty-Free/Corbis, (8) Charles A. Blakeslee/age fotostock, (9) Royalty-Free/Corbis; p. 107 (background) Gary Braasch/Getty Images, (top) Joel W. Rogers/Corbis, (left) Tom Brakefield/The Image Works, (bottom) Bob Daemmrich/The Image Works; p. 113 Plush Studios/Getty Images; p. 114 Bettmann/Corbis; p. 116 Images.com/Corbis; p. 117 (top) erikdegraaf/Shutterstock.com, (middle) Kazuyoshi Nomachi/Corbis, (bottom) James Morgan/Shutterstock.com; p. 118 (top left) PA News Photos, (top right) Gary Hershorn/Reuters/Corbis, (bottom left) Koichi Kamoshida/Getty Images, (bottom right) Timothy A. Clary/Getty Images; p. 119 (left) Royalty-Free/Corbis, (middle) Corbis, (right) Mark Allan/Alpha/Globe Photos; p. 120 Rubberball/Jupiterimages; p. 121 Sean Kiel/Workbook Stock/Jupiterimages, (background) Mr Funkenstien/Shutterstock.com; p. 123 (top to bottom) Gary Conner/Index Stock Imagery, Fujifotos/The Image Works, Robert Holmes/Corbis, Peter M. Wilson/Corbis; p. 124 (middle) Hinata Haga/HAGA/The Image Works, (bottom) Peter Sanders/HAGA/The Image Works; p. 125 (top) Ariel Skelley/Corbis; p. 126 (left) Anthony Cassidy/Getty Images, (right) David Young-Wolff/PhotoEdit, (bottom) David Young-Wolff/PhotoEdit; p. 127 Dave Bartruff/Corbis; 128 (top) Buzz Pictures/Alamy, (bottom) Andres Kudacki/Corbis; p. 129 Michael Steele/Getty Images.

ii

Contents

Scope and Sequence	iv
Characters	viii
Let's get started.	2
UNIT 1 Welcome to California.	6
UNIT 2 Did you bring the brochure?	14
Progress check	21
Game 1	22
Project 1	23
UNIT 3 You like him, don't you?	24
Wide Angle 1	32
UNIT 4 I've been sitting here …	34
Progress check	41
UNIT 5 The bigger the waves, …	42
Game 2	50
Project 2	51
UNIT 6 Will you be needing it later?	52
Progress check	59
Wide Angle 2	60
UNIT 7 If I were you, I'd …	62
UNIT 8 I hadn't seen him in years.	70
Progress check	77
Game 3	78
Project 3	79
UNIT 9 Mom said I had to go.	80
Wide Angle 3	88
UNIT 10 He's not good enough to win.	90
Progress check	97
UNIT 11 Solutions were discussed.	98
Game 4	106
Project 4	107
UNIT 12 Even though he's arrogant, …	108
Progress check	115
Wide Angle 4	116
Fun with songs 1–4	118
Focus on culture 1–4	122
Fun with grammar	130
Peer editing checklist	134
Word list	135

Scope and Sequence

Unit	Title	Communication	Grammar
Pages 2–5	Let's get started.		
1 Pages 6–13	Welcome to California.	Make small talk	The simple present and the present continuous Infinitive of purpose (*to* + the base form of a verb)
2 Pages 14–20	Did you bring the brochure?	Ask for information about transportation	*The* or no article before nouns The simple past - Affirmative and negative statements - *Yes/No* questions - Information questions The present perfect and the simple past
Page 21	Progress check Units 1 and 2 Test-taking tip: Start preparing for your tests early.		
Page 22 Page 23	Game 1: Why pie Project 1: A snapshot of transportation		
3 Pages 24–31	You like him, don't you?	Confirm information	*Should/Shouldn't; Had better/Had better not* Tag questions with *be* Tag questions with *do*
Pages 32–33	Wide Angle 1: Surfing: Hawaiian Style		
4 Pages 34–40	I've been sitting here …	Express regret	The present perfect and the present perfect continuous *Should have/Shouldn't have*
Page 41	Progress check Units 3 and 4 Test-taking tip: Join a study group.		
5 Pages 42–49	The bigger the waves, …	Make comparisons	Comparative and superlative forms of adverbs Comparatives with *a lot*, *far*, and *much* Double comparatives: *the . . . the*
Page 50 Page 51	Game 2: Tag relay Project 2: A snapshot of pros and cons		
6 Pages 52–58	Will you be needing it later?	Talk about future possibilities in technology	The future: *will* + verb and *be going to* + verb The future continuous: *will be* + verb *-ing*
Page 59	Progress check Units 5 and 6 Test-taking tip: Don't get stuck on one item.		
Pages 60–61	Wide Angle 2: Emotional Electronics		

iv   Scope and Sequence

Vocabulary	Skills	Learn to learn	Pronunciation
Nouns derived from verbs	*Reading*: Read for specific information *Listening*: Listen for specific information *Speaking*: Introduce oneself; Initiate a conversation and make small talk *Writing*: Write a conversation	Talk with native speakers of English	Syllable stress
Means of transportation	*Reading*: Read for specific information *Listening*: Listen to a description of a place *Speaking*: Ask for information/directions *Writing*: Write a descriptive paragraph about a place	Ask for confirmation and clarification	Sounds of *the*
Expressions with *get*	*Reading*: Read for general information *Listening*: Listen for intonation to determine the speaker's intention *Speaking*: Express opinions *Writing*: Give advice in writing	Skim for the main idea	Intonation patterns in tag questions
Adjective to noun transformation	*Reading*: Read for specific information *Listening*: Listen for specific information *Speaking*: Describe cultural behaviors; Give advice *Writing*: Write a fictional paragraph about what you have been doing	Understand other cultures	Reduced forms: *should have* and *shouldn't have*
Word building	*Reading*: Read for specific information *Listening*: Listen for specific information *Speaking*: Express and defend opinions; Make comparisons *Writing*: Write the results of a discussion in chart form; Write a conversation	Build vocabulary using visualization	Use intonation for emphasis
Computer terms	*Reading*: Read a timeline *Listening*: Listen for specific information *Speaking*: Talk about future possibilities; Express opinions; Ask and answer questions about a trip *Writing*: Write about resolutions and predictions; Write a public announcement	Review your writing goals	Stress in phrasal verbs

Scope and Sequence

Scope and Sequence

Unit	Title	Communication	Grammar
7 Pages 62–69	*If I were you, I'd …*	Talk about imaginary situations	First conditional: *If* clauses in future-time situations Second conditional: *If* clauses in imaginary situations *I wish* + the simple past: Expressing wishes for a present situation
8 Pages 70–76	*I hadn't seen him in years.*	Talk about a past incident	The past perfect - Affirmative and negative statements - *Yes/No* questions The past perfect and the simple past: Expressing the relationship between two past events
Page 77	Progress check Units 7 and 8	Test-taking tip: Don't get too nervous.	
Page 78 Page 79	Game 3: Imagination Project 3: A snapshot of my ideal world		
9 Pages 80–87	*Mom said I had to go.*	Report what someone has said	Reported speech - Statements - Questions - Using *said* and *told*
Pages 88–89	Wide Angle 3: Teens Taking Action		
10 Pages 90–96	*He's not good enough to win.*	Express disappointment	*Too* + adjective/adverb + *to* (*not*) + adjective/adverb + *enough to* *So* + a clause of result *Such* + a clause of result
Page 97	Progress check Units 9 and 10	Test-taking tip: Don't make assumptions.	
11 Pages 98–105	*Solutions were discussed.*	Ask for information by telephone	The passive voice: Statements The passive voice: Questions - *Yes/No* questions - Information questions
Page 106 Page 107	Game 4: Gossip Project 4: A snapshot of a global issue		
12 Pages 108–114	*Even though he's arrogant,…*	Express pleasure and thanks	Connectors: Showing addition with *and*, contrast with *but*, result with *so*, and condition with *or* Showing contrast with *although/even though*, *in spite of*, and *however*
Page 115	Progress check Units 11 and 12	Test-taking tip: Learn from your previous tests.	
Pages 116–117	Wide Angle 4: It's Getting Hot in Here.		

Vocabulary	Skills	Learn to learn	Pronunciation
Phrasal verbs with *go*	*Reading*: Read for specific information *Listening*: Make inferences based on questions *Speaking*: Talk about wishes; Discuss changing the world *Writing*: Write about dreams, wishes, and future possibilities	Find definitions in a dictionary	Intonation in sentences with *if* clauses
Word building with verbs of emotion	*Reading*: Read for specific information *Listening*: Listen for specific information *Speaking*: Talk about the past; Talk about entertainment (movies, actors, etc.) *Writing*: Write about a person you admire	Make predictions	Reduction of function words
Idioms	*Reading*: Read for specific information *Listening*: Take notes from a phoned-in message; Listen for specific information *Speaking*: Report what someone has said *Writing*: Write about family reunions	Keep a vocabulary notebook	Intonation in quoted and reported speech
Strong adjectives	*Reading*: Find synonyms for words in a reading *Listening*: Make inferences; Listen for tone *Speaking*: Express opinions; Express disappointment *Writing*: Write about what you will do when you're old enough	Find the right word	Emphatic stress with *so* and *such*
Environmental issues The natural environment	*Reading*: Interpret an environmental map *Listening*: Listen for specific information; Draw conclusions from a radio advertisement *Speaking*: Discuss environmental issues and suggest solutions *Writing*: Write about an environmental issue	Revise your writing	Sentence stress
Personality traits	*Reading*: Read for specific and general information *Listening*: Listen for general information *Speaking*: Express opinions; Express thanks; Talk about personalities *Writing*: Write a paragraph about an inspirational person	Find the main idea: topic sentences	Use intonation to show contrast

Scope and Sequence   vii

Let's get started.

Vocabulary

1 Adjectives and their antonyms

A. Complete the antonyms (opposites).

1. ugly — b <u>eautiful</u>
2. boring — i _____
3. professional — u _____
4. impatient — p _____
5. clean — d _____
6. pleasant — u _____
7. quiet — n _____
8. rich — p _____
9. heavy — l _____
10. comfortable — u _____

B. **A2** Listen and repeat as you check your answers.

2 School subjects

A. Write the names of the school subjects under the correct pictures.

history	literature	music	science
languages	math	physical education (P.E.)	~~social studies~~

1. <u>social studies</u>

2. _____

3. _____

4. _____

5. _____

6. _____

7. _____

8. _____

B. **PAIRS.** Make a list of other subjects you study. Then share it with another pair.

- Biology
  Algebra
- Design and Technology

2 Let's get started.

3 Occupations

A. The words for the occupations shown below are all in the puzzle. Find them and write them in the blanks.

T	E	A	C	O	N	D	U	C	T	O	R
S	A	I	L	O	R	O	R	E	E	B	A
A	H	A	N	O	D	C	E	M	A	A	T
C	S	E	A	L	O	T	P	R	C	K	E
T	E	B	A	K	L	O	E	R	H	E	K
O	O	G	T	N	D	R	I	V	E	R	R
R	E	S	I	S	I	N	G	E	R	Y	U

1. _____actor_____

2. _____

3. _____

4. _____

5. _____

6. _____

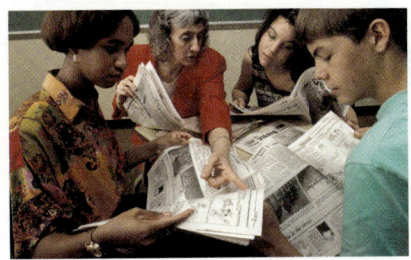
7. _____

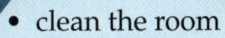
8. _____

B. PAIRS. Do you know any other words for occupations, (for example, *dentist, bank clerk*)? Do you know people who do any of these jobs? Tell your partner about them.

For example:

My neighbor, Mrs. da Silva, is a pharmacist.
My friend's father is a taxi driver.

4 Household chores

A. Read the phrases.

- clean the room
- clear the table
- cook lunch (or dinner)
- do the grocery shopping
- do the laundry
- iron the clothes
- make the bed
- vacuum the floor
- wash the dishes

B. PAIRS. Ask each other the following questions.

- Which household chores do you have to do?
- Which ones do you like doing? Which ones do you hate doing?

For example:

I have to wash the dishes . . .
I like cooking lunch, but I hate . . .

Let's get started. 3

Grammar

1 The simple past and present perfect

A. Write the simple past and past participle forms.

Base form	Simple past	Past participle
be	was/were	been
buy		bought
do	did	
go	went	
have		had
know		
leave		
see		

B. Write questions using the present perfect.
1. A: *Have you had lunch yet?*
   B: Yes, I have. I had a sandwich at one o'clock.
2. A: _____
   B: Yes, I have. I saw the movie last Saturday.
3. A: _____
   B: No, I haven't. I've been to Florida, but not to California.

2 Verb forms

A. Read the verb forms and the sentences.

Form	Sample sentence
simple present:	I usually **leave** for school at 7:00 A.M.
simple past:	I **caught** the bus at 7:30 this morning.
present continuous:	I'**m wearing** my new jeans.
past continuous:	I **was reading** when the teacher came in the room.
present perfect:	I'**ve been** here since nine o'clock.
future with *will*:	I'**ll see** you later.
future with *be going to*:	It'**s going to** rain.

B. **GROUPS.** Play a game. Follow the instructions.
1. Stand in a circle. S1 (Student 1) is holding a soft ball for tossing. S1 says the first sentence in the chart, but revises it with his or her own information. For example, "I usually leave for school at 6:30 A.M." Then S1 tosses the ball to S2.
2. S2 says the sentence but revises it with his or her own information. S2 then tosses the ball to S3. Repeat the process.
3. After five students have made their own sentences, go on to the next sentence in the chart, and repeat the process. Do this with the first five sentences in the chart.

3 Comparative and superlative forms of adjectives

A. Complete the chart.

Adjective	Comparative adjective	Superlative adjective
1. good	*better than*	
2.		the closest
3.	more difficult than	
4.		the most talented
5. fast		
6.	taller than	

B. Choose one of the adjectives from the chart. Write three sentences. Follow the example.

tall   *My dad is tall.*
         My dad is taller than my mom.
         My big brother is the tallest person in our family.

_____   _____
          _____
          _____

4   Let's get started.

Communication

1 Responding to questions

Match the questions and the appropriate responses.

____ 1. Would you please take out the trash?
____ 2. Have you ever seen a panda?
____ 3. Can I help you?
____ 4. Would you like to go to the movies Friday?
____ 5. Did you use to study German?
____ 6. Excuse me. Can you tell me the time?

a. No, I haven't. But I'd like to see one.
b. Yes, it's 10:45.
c. Sure. No problem.
d. Yes. Can you tell me where the exit is?
e. Sure. That sounds like fun.
f. Yes, I did. But I switched to Italian.

2 Saying the right thing

Write the appropriate expressions. Use words from the box.

| I know. | Oh, well. | Really? | ~~Same here.~~ | That's OK. |

Say this when . . .

1. you feel the same way as someone else. " _____Same here._____ "
2. something is wrong or not good, but nothing can be done about it. " _____ "
3. someone says something, and you already knew about it. " _____ "
4. you're surprised by what someone has said. " _____ "
5. someone apologizes, and you want to accept his or her apology. " _____ "

3 Having a discussion

A. Review the useful language commonly used in discussions.

- I agree.
- I disagree.
- I think . . .
- I don't think . . .
- What do you think?
- I'm not sure about that.
- If you ask me . . .
- That's a good point.
- I'm sorry. Could you say that again, please?

B. GROUPS. Play a game. Follow the instructions.

Place a small bowl in the center of your group. Hold three coins or beans in your hand. Discuss the topics below. Each time you use one of the phrases, put one of your coins or beans into the bowl. When all three of your coins or beans are in the bowl, you can drop out of the conversation.

Possible topics:

- Who's the best singer?
- What's the best band?
- What's the best song?
- Who's the best soccer player in the world?
- Which soccer team is the best in the world?
- What's the best movie showing right now in movie theaters?
- What's the best movie ever?

Let's get started. 5

1 Welcome to California.

1 Reading

A3 Read along as you listen.

California
THE GOLDEN STATE

California. This beautiful state is home to more than 35 million people, representing a variety of races, cultures, and languages. Most Californians are descendants of European immigrants, but more than a quarter of them have ethnic roots in Spain and Latin America. Millions more come from Asia.

Many of these people moved to California during the Gold Rush. They came hoping to get rich. Some succeeded, some did not.

So why are people still moving to California? Because it is still a place where dreams come true. Right this minute, hundreds of young people who want to become movie or TV stars are leaving home, headed for Hollywood.

San Diego, in southern California, is another popular destination. People are attracted to San Diego because of its beautiful, mild weather and great beaches.

Then there's Silicon Valley, the area between San Francisco and Santa Cruz. During the technology boom in the mid-1990s, Silicon Valley became a center of technological research and development. Large numbers of people moved to the area, looking for jobs in technology.

Today, California continues to attract people from all over the world. It remains a land of opportunity.

Learning goals
Communication
Make small talk

Grammar
The simple present and the present continuous
Infinitive of purpose

Vocabulary
Nouns derived from verbs

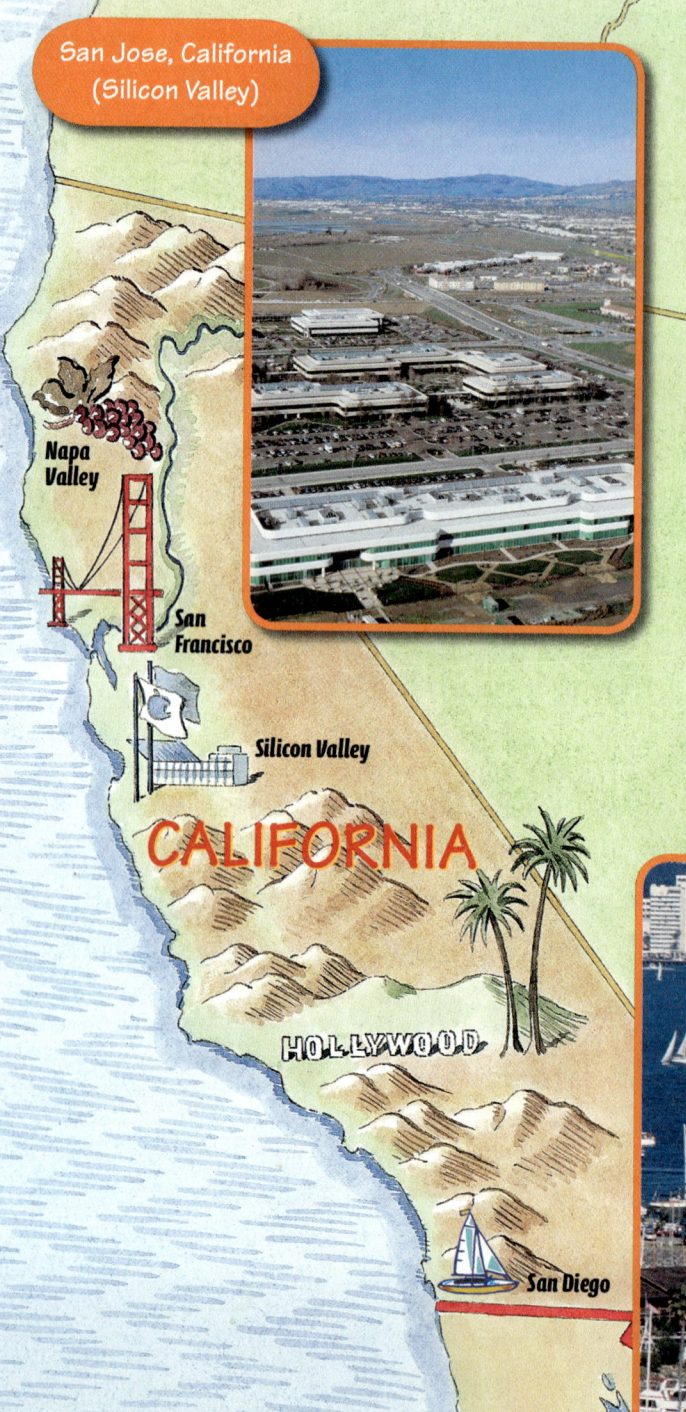

2 Comprehension

Answer the questions.

1. Where do many Californians come from?
2. Why are people moving to Hollywood and San Diego?
3. Why did people move to Silicon Valley in the 1990s?

Unit 1

GRAMMAR FOCUS

The simple present and the present continuous

I usually **wait** for the bus here.
I **am waiting** for the bus right now.

People **move** to California every day.
Today, people **are moving** to California.

The sun often **shines** in San Diego.
The sun **is shining** now.

Verbs not normally used in the present continuous:
be, feel, hate, have, hear, know, like, look, love, need, remember, see, think, want

Discovering grammar

Look at the grammar chart. Answer the questions.

1. Which tense do you use to talk about something that is happening right now?
   the present continuous
2. What ending is added to the verb in the present continuous? _____
3. What ending sometimes gets added to the verb in the simple present? _____
4. Read the list of words not normally used in the present continuous. Cover the list, and write four of the words here:
   _____, _____,
   _____, _____

Practicing grammar

3 Practice

Fill in the blanks with the simple present or the present continuous form of the verb in parentheses. You may use contractions.

I can't believe I (1. sit) **'m sitting** in my classroom right now. I had to stay after class with my teacher to do my homework. I usually (2. do) _____ all my homework before class. But not this time. I (3. hate) _____ staying after class.

My teacher (4. read) _____ a book. She's a very intelligent person, so she (5. read) _____ a lot. I admire that in a person.

There's that spider again. What's it (6. do) _____? It (7. move) _____ really fast. Ah, it (8. spin) _____ a new web. . . . Oh, good. Time's up. Bye!

4 Practice

Have a competition! Go to page 130.

5 Listening

A4 Listen to the conversation. Then circle the correct answers.

1. Charlie is at (*his house* / *Jason's house*).
2. Jason is (*listening to music* / *cleaning*).
3. Evan is (*skateboarding* / *playing soccer*) in the park.
4. Jason locked his little brother in (*his bedroom* / *the bathroom*).
5. Jason's little brother is cleaning the door with a (*toothbrush* / *hairbrush*).

San Diego, California

Unit 1 7

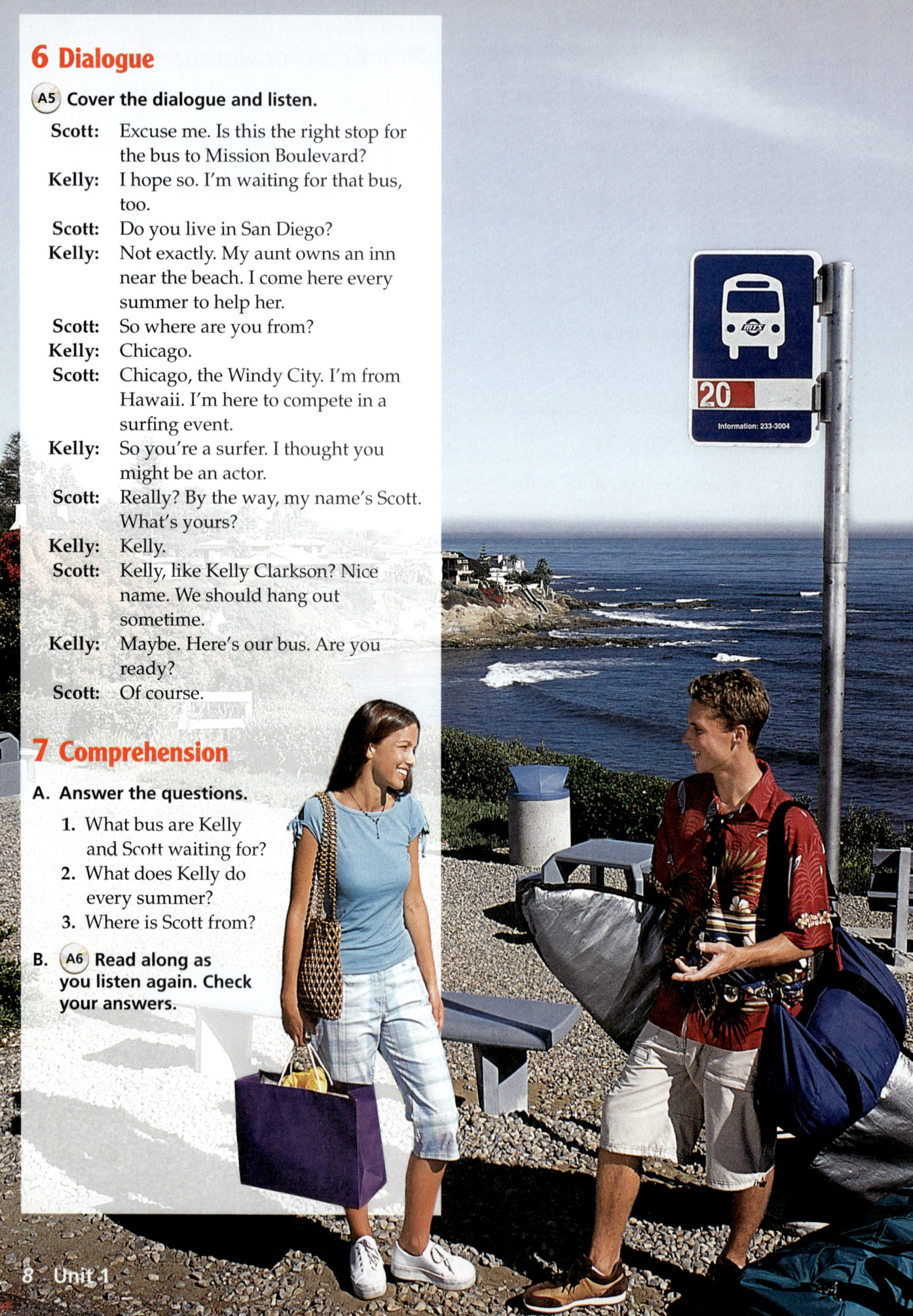

6 Dialogue

A5 Cover the dialogue and listen.

Scott: Excuse me. Is this the right stop for the bus to Mission Boulevard?
Kelly: I hope so. I'm waiting for that bus, too.
Scott: Do you live in San Diego?
Kelly: Not exactly. My aunt owns an inn near the beach. I come here every summer to help her.
Scott: So where are you from?
Kelly: Chicago.
Scott: Chicago, the Windy City. I'm from Hawaii. I'm here to compete in a surfing event.
Kelly: So you're a surfer. I thought you might be an actor.
Scott: Really? By the way, my name's Scott. What's yours?
Kelly: Kelly.
Scott: Kelly, like Kelly Clarkson? Nice name. We should hang out sometime.
Kelly: Maybe. Here's our bus. Are you ready?
Scott: Of course.

7 Comprehension

A. Answer the questions.

1. What bus are Kelly and Scott waiting for?
2. What does Kelly do every summer?
3. Where is Scott from?

B. **A6** Read along as you listen again. Check your answers.

8 Unit 1

8 Useful expressions

A. **A7** Listen and repeat.
- I hope so.
- Not exactly.
- Of course.

B. Fill in the blanks. Use the expressions in Exercise A.

1. **Situation:** There's an empty seat next to you.
   A: Can I sit here?
   B: *Of course.*

2. **Situation:** You've lived in California for a long time, but you were born somewhere else.
   A: Are you from California?
   B: _____

3. **Situation:** You're waiting for the bus. You have to get home quickly.
   A: Is the next bus coming soon?
   B: _____ I'm in a hurry.

C. **PAIRS.** Practice the conversations in Exercise B.

9 Vocabulary

Nouns derived from verbs

A. **A8** Some nouns can be formed by adding *-er*, *-or*, or *-r* to the main verb. Look at the chart. Listen and repeat the nouns.

verb	+ suffix	= noun
1. surf	-er	surf**er**
2. act	-or	act**or**
3. bake	-r	bake**r**

Note: With some words, you have to double the final consonant: run/run**ner**.

B. Use your dictionary to find the nouns for the people who do these things. Write the nouns in the spaces.

1. sing   *singer*
2. write _____
3. edit   _____
4. build _____
5. drive _____
6. drum   _____

10 Pronunciation

Syllable stress

A. **A9** Listen. Notice the stressed syllables in each word.

<u>sur</u>fer   Chi<u>ca</u>go   com<u>pete</u>   inter<u>na</u>tional

B. **A10** Listen and repeat. Underline the syllable that receives the most stress.

1. driver
2. conductor
3. teenager
4. exactly
5. excuse me
6. actor
7. compete
8. competition
9. entertainer
10. entertainment
11. technical
12. technology

C. **A11** **PAIRS.** Listen and repeat. Then practice the conversations.

1. A: Excuse me. I think I know you. Are you an actor?
   B: No, I'm not. But everyone says I look like Orlando Bloom.

2. A: Is your dad good with technical things?
   B: Not really. He's hopeless with technology.

3. A: Do you think teenagers are good drivers?
   B: Not exactly . . . well, some are, I guess.

Unit 1   9

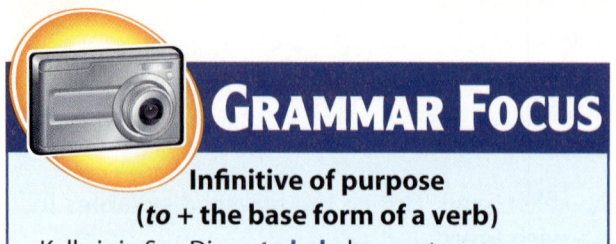

GRAMMAR FOCUS

Infinitive of purpose
(*to* + the base form of a verb)
Kelly is in San Diego **to help** her aunt.
Scott came here **to compete** in a surfing event.

Discovering grammar

Look at the grammar chart. Circle the correct answers.

1. What question does an infinitive of purpose often answer?
   a. *Why?*   b. *What?*
2. What word comes before the base form of a verb to make the infinitive?
   a. a form of *be*   b. *to*
3. What is an example of an infinitive of purpose?
   a. *She's in the United States to learn English.*
   b. *She wants to learn English.*

Practicing grammar

11 Practice

Answer the questions. Use the phrase in parentheses in an infinitive of purpose.

1. Why is Maria going to town? (*buy some flowers*)
   She's going to town to buy some flowers.
2. Why does Rob practice basketball every day? (*become a good player*)
   _____
   _____
3. Why is Kendra traveling to Brazil this summer? (*visit her cousins*)
   _____
   _____
4. Why does José Luis work at the store on Saturdays? (*earn some money for his vacation*)
   _____
   _____

12 Practice

Carrie just got her first job. Look at her list of things to do before the first day. Then answer the questions. Make your sentences complete.

- call Grandma; tell about new job
- go on computer; read bus schedule
- go to mall; buy new shoes
- go to bank with Mom; get money
- call new boss; find out next week's schedule

1. Why did Carrie call her grandma?
   She called her grandma to tell her about her new job.
2. Why did she go on the computer?
   _____
   _____
3. Why did she go to the mall?
   _____
   _____
4. Why did she go to the bank with her mom?
   _____
   _____
5. Why did she call her new boss?
   _____
   _____

10 Unit 1

13 Practice

Read the teenagers' statements. Combine each pair of sentences using infinitives of purpose. Write the new sentences.

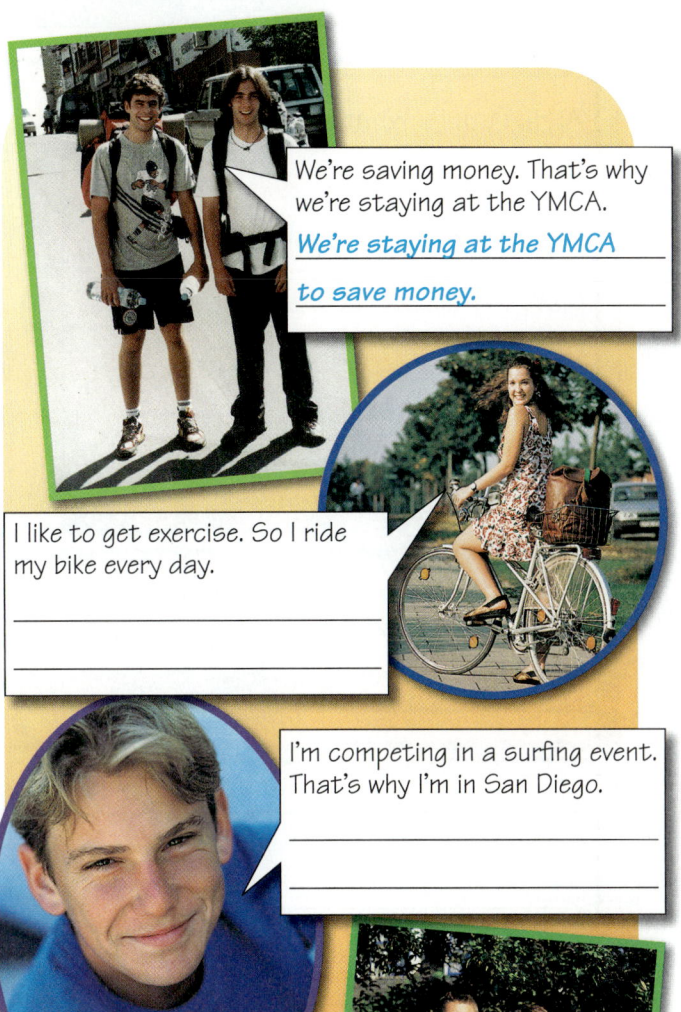

We're saving money. That's why we're staying at the YMCA.
We're staying at the YMCA to save money.

I like to get exercise. So I ride my bike every day.
_____
_____

I'm competing in a surfing event. That's why I'm in San Diego.
_____
_____

We're visiting relatives. That's why we're in Canada.
_____
_____

I want to make some money. So I'm working at a restaurant.
_____
_____

14 Your turn

A. Write two sentences. Then combine them to make a new sentence with an infinitive of purpose.

For example:
He's getting ready for a big exam on Monday. That's why he's studying in the library on a Saturday.

He's studying in the library on a Saturday to get ready for a big exam on Monday.

She's _____
_____
_____

She's _____
_____
_____

B. **PAIRS.** Share your sentences with a classmate.

Unit 1 11

15 Communication

Make small talk

A. 🎧 **Listen and read.**

  A: So you're here to visit relatives. Do you like California?
  B: I love it!
  A: Really? What do you like about it?
  B: There are tons of things to do, especially here in San Diego.
  A: Like?
  B: Well, you can go to the beach anytime. And, of course, you can go to theme parks. What about you? Don't you like it here?
  A: I'm not sure yet.

B. **PAIRS.** Write a conversation similar to the one in Exercise A. To keep the conversation going, use expressions like these: *Really? What do you like about it? Like? What about you?*

C. **GROUPS.** Role-play your new conversation in front of another pair.

Learn to learn

Talk with native speakers of English.

Use every opportunity to have a conversation in English with native speakers.

A. **PAIRS.** Think of "small talk" you could use to help you start a conversation with a native speaker of English. Make a list of conversation starters and memorize them. Here are a few ideas:

- Is this your first time in . . .
- Is this seat free?
- I like your . . .
- That's a cool . . .

B. Look for interviews in English magazines. Practice reading them aloud to help you feel more confident when asking people questions.

16 Writing

A. Dennis and his friend are IMing each other. Read their conversation below.

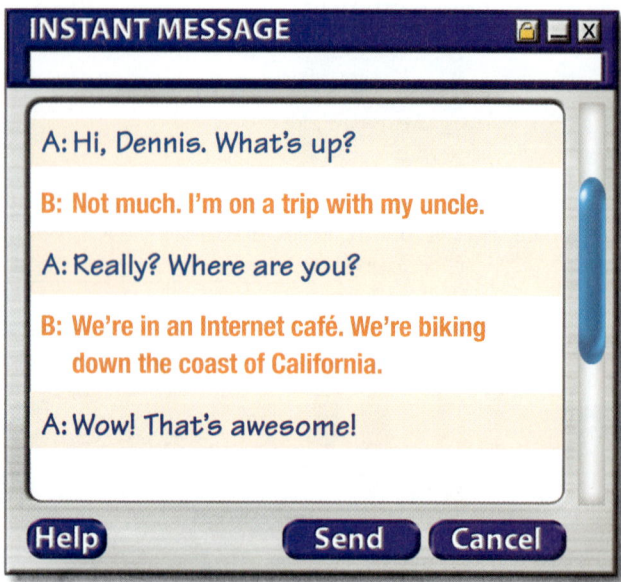

B. **PAIRS.** Write an instant message conversation like the one in Exercise A.

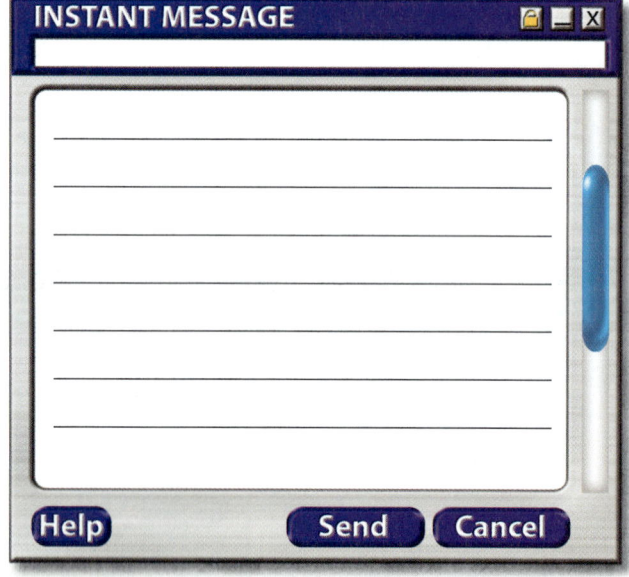

GROUPS. What do you and your friends like to talk about when you're online? Talk about it.

Useful language:
- What things do you usually talk about?
- Most of the time I . . .
- I sometimes . . .
- Same here.
- Not me.

12 Unit 1

Putting it together Meeting Jack and Denise

A. **A13** Read along as you listen. Who's going to work at the inn with Kelly? Jack or Denise?

B. **GROUPS.** Answer the questions.
1. What does Aunt Paula notice about Kelly at the beginning of the conversation?
2. What does Jack ask when he arrives?
3. Why did Denise come to the inn?

Unit 1   13

2 Did you bring the brochure?

1 Dialogue

A14 Cover the dialogue and listen.

Denise: So, Jack, did you bring the brochure?
Jack: Of course I did. Here you go.
Denise: Thanks. By the way, Kelly, we're planning to go to Universal Studios. Would you like to come along?
Kelly: Sure. How do we get there? By bus?
Jack: No, I'll drive. We can go to the Hollywood Walk of Fame, too.
Kelly: Sounds like a plan. Let me check out my work schedule and see which days I'm free. Uh-oh. Look who's here!
Jack: Who? The guy with the blond hair?
Kelly: Yeah. He's the surfer from Hawaii I told you about.

Kelly: Scott! What are you doing here?
Scott: I heard your aunt serves great pancakes. Nice place you've got here.
Kelly: Thanks. How did you find it?
Scott: I asked around. So where's my table?

Learning goals

Communication
Ask for information about transportation

Grammar
The or no article before nouns
The simple past
The present perfect and the simple past

Vocabulary
Means of transportation

2 Comprehension

A. Answer the questions.

1. Where are the three friends planning to go?
2. What reason did Scott give for showing up at the inn?
3. What do you think was the real reason for his visit?

B. **A15** Read along as you listen again. Check your answers.

3 Useful expressions

A. **A16** Listen and repeat.
- Here you go.
- check out
- Sounds like a plan.
- Uh-oh!

B. **PAIRS.** Replace each underlined phrase with a phrase from Exercise A. Then practice the new dialogue.

A: Can I see your magazine?
B: Sure. <u>Here you are.</u>
A: Hey, <u>look at</u> this picture, guys!
B: Be careful! The coffee . . . ! <u>Oh, no!</u>
A: I'm sorry. Let's walk to the store. I'll get you a new magazine.
B: <u>I like your idea.</u>

4 Vocabulary

Means of transportation

A. **A17** Listen and repeat.

1. plane
2. bike
3. boat
4. bus
5. car
6. ferry
7. helicopter
8. motorcycle
9. ship
10. taxi
11. train
12. truck

B. **PAIRS.** Think of a place in your area. Quiz your classmate on ways to get there. Use these phrases.
- to go by car/taxi/bus/train/boat/air
- to take a taxi/bus/train/boat
- to walk/ride a bike/fly/drive

A: Tell me four ways to get from here to the library.
B: You can walk, you can ride a bike, you can go by car, or you can take a bus.

5 Communication

Ask for information about transportation

A. **A18** Listen and read.

A: Excuse me. How can I get to the art museum from here?
B: You can go by bus or by train. The bus takes 20 minutes and the train takes 10 minutes.
A: Thanks. I think I'll take the train.

B. **PAIRS.** Role-play the conversation. Substitute the art museum with a place in your area.

Unit 2

GRAMMAR FOCUS

The or no article before nouns

The (specific)
Here's **the** surfer from Hawaii.
Here are **the** brochures you wanted.

No article (general)
Surfers are cool.
Brochures offer useful information about a place.

Note: Use *the* with the names of hotels, theaters, some countries, and geographical features and regions; for example, *the Hilton Hotel*, *the Himalayas*, *the Atlantic Ocean*.

Discovering grammar

Look at the grammar chart. Circle the correct answer.

The article *the* goes with nouns that (*are* / *aren't*) specific.

Practicing grammar

6 Practice

Complete the sentences using the cues.

1. (cartoons)
   a. Do you watch ____the cartoons____ that are on channel 5?
   b. ____Cartoons____ are not just for kids.
2. (music)
   a. _____ I downloaded was awesome.
   b. We listen to _____ when we do our homework.
3. (schools)
   a. Like it or not, _____ have rules to keep kids safe.
   b. _____ we go to have a lot of rules, don't they?
4. (sneakers)
   a. _____ are dirty.
   b. _____ can cost a lot, so shop carefully.

7 Pronunciation

Sounds of *the*

A. **A19** Listen and repeat.

the/the best pizza   the/the Internet

B. **A20** Listen and repeat.
   1. the wrong information   the information
   2. the blue ocean   the ocean
   3. the thick envelope   the envelope

C. **A21** **PAIRS.** Listen and repeat.
   1. Let's get mom the expensive earrings, not the cheap ones.
   2. We washed the outside of the car, but we didn't clean the inside.
   3. The solar system is small in comparison to the universe.

GRAMMAR FOCUS

The simple past

Affirmative statements
Denise **invited** Kelly to Universal Studios.
Jack **brought** the brochure.

Negative statements
Denise **didn't invite** Kelly to the zoo.
Scott **didn't bring** the brochure.

Yes/No questions   **Short answers**
Did Denise **invite** Kelly?   Yes, she **did**.
Did Scott **bring** the brochure?   No, he **didn't**.

Information questions
Where **did** Denise **invite** Kelly?
What **did** Jack **bring**?

Note: The past tense forms of irregular verbs vary. You have to memorize them.

Discovering grammar

Look at the grammar chart. Circle the correct answers.

1. In negative statements, use *didn't* + (*the base form* / *simple past form*) of the verb.
2. In *Yes/No* questions, use *Did* + (*the base form* / *the simple past form*) of the verb.

Unit 2

Practicing grammar

8 Practice

PAIRS. Fill in the blanks with the simple past form of the verbs in parentheses.

Walt Disney, Ruler of the Magic Kingdom™

Everyone knows the name Walt Disney. He's the man who (1. *create*) __created__ Mickey Mouse, (2. *make*) _____ the first animated movie, and (3. *invent*) _____ the Disney Theme Parks. But not everyone knows about Disney's difficult past.

Disney and his brothers (4. *grow*) _____ up in poverty. Young Walt (5. *find*) _____ a way to forget his problems through his art classes. He (6. *leave*) _____ home at the age of sixteen and (7. *join*) _____ the Red Cross, serving in World War I. After the war, he (8. *open*) _____ an art shop in Kansas City, Missouri. There he (9. *learn*) _____ the art of animation, a new field at the time.

Disney's life (10. *continue*) _____ to be difficult. He (11. *live*) _____ at the studio where he (12. *work*) _____, and he (13. *eat*) _____ cold beans out of a can. But his luck (14. *begin*) _____ to change when he (15. *move*) _____ to Los Angeles and (16. *take*) _____ his brother Roy as a business partner.

It was then, in an era of silent movies, that Disney's Mickey Mouse (17. *appear*) _____ singing a tune. Sound films were just starting, and a movie with music (18. *be*) _____ big news. The public (19. *love*) _____ it. At the time of his death in 1966, Disney (20. *have*) _____ thirty Oscars, wealth, and the adoration of millions of children all over the world.

9 Practice

In your notebook, write six *Yes/No* questions and short answers about Exercise 8.

For example:

Did Disney create Mickey Mouse?

Yes, he did.

Did Disney have an easy life?

No, he didn't.

B. PAIRS. Exchange questions with your classmate. Answer each other's questions without looking at your books. Who got the most correct answers?

10 Practice

A. In your notebook, write six information questions about Exercise 8.

For example:

What kind of childhood did Disney have?

Unit 2 17

GRAMMAR FOCUS

The present perfect and the simple past

The present perfect (indefinite time)
I **have been** to California many times.
People **have** always **loved** Mickey Mouse.
My brother **has** never **flown** in a plane.
Have you ever **ridden** a trolley car?

The simple past (specific time)
I **was** in California last year.
People **loved** the first Mickey Mouse movie.
My brother **didn't fly** to Orlando last month; he **took** a train.
Did you **ride** the trolley car or **take** a taxi?

Discovering grammar

Look at the grammar chart. Circle the correct answers.

1. The present perfect is used for (*specific / indefinite*) time.
2. The simple past is used for (*specific / indefinite*) time.
3. The present perfect is made by combining (*have / be*) with the past participle form of a verb.

Practicing grammar

11 Practice

Circle the correct answers.

1. I (*took* / *have taken*) the trolley car to Chinatown a few days ago.
2. He (*wanted* / *has wanted*) a new bicycle for some time.
3. My sister (*got* / *has gotten*) her driver's license yesterday, so now she can drive.
4. My neighbors and I (*took* / *have taken*) the bus to school together since we were in first grade.
5. I (*haven't flown* / *didn't fly*) in a helicopter before.
6. They (*rode* / *have ridden*) their motorcycles down to Florida last summer.

13 Practice

Fill in the blanks with the verbs in parentheses. Use the present perfect or the simple past.

A: How long have you been here?

B: I (1. *be*) _____have been_____ here for about three weeks. I (2. *arrive*) _____ on the fifteenth.

A: What have you done since you got here?

B: I (3. *eat*) _____ out a lot. As a matter of fact, I (4. *eat*) _____ at a really good place last night. I want to go there again.

A: Have you been to the mall?

B: I (5. *be*) _____ there this morning, actually. Yes, I (6. *be*) _____ there lots of times.

A: Are you going to the movies again this weekend?

B: I (7. *not/decide*) _____ yet. I (8. *seen*) _____ a lot of movies recently. I think I might just stay home.

12 Practice

Have a competition! Go to page 130.

18 Unit 2

14 Your turn

A. **PAIRS.** Trade books with your classmate. In your classmate's book, complete the "places" column. Then trade books back and complete the rest of the chart with your own information.

Places	Have you ever been to...	If yes, when did you go?
A famous amusement park: Disneyland	yes	two summers ago
A famous zoo:		
A famous museum:		
A famous city:		
Other:		

B. **PAIRS.** Talk about your completed chart with your classmate.

Your classmate: Have you ever been to . . . ?
You: Yes, I have.
Your classmate: Oh, really? When did you go?
You: We went two summers ago. I went with my family . . .

GROUPS. Make a list of tourist attractions you've heard of or been to. Then talk about them.

Useful language:
- I've always wanted to go to _____.
- Have you ever been to _____?
- Would you ever go there again?
- What did you think of it?
- It was great/not so good/pretty boring.
- So, which one was your favorite?

15 Listening

A22 Listen to the conversation. Then answer the questions.

1. Where are Alicia and her mom going?
   _____

2. What does Alicia want to do?
   _____

3. Complete the chart for their old reservation and new reservation:

Old Reservation		New Reservation	
Departure date:	_____	Departure date:	_____
Departure time:	10:15 A.M.	Departure time:	_____
Return date:	May 6th	Return date:	_____
Return time:	_____	Return time:	_____

Learn to learn

Ask for confirmation and clarification.

Knowing how to ask for confirmation and clarification is an important strategy for comprehension and learning.

A23 Listen to the conversation in Exercise 15 again. Listen to the ways the speakers ask for confirmation or clarification. Check them off as you hear them.

Confirmation
☐ From Los Angeles to San Diego?
☐ That was May 10th?
☐ Is 4:30 still OK?

Clarification
☐ What's the fare again?
☐ You mean the 11th, right?

16 Reading

A24 How well do you know California? Listen and read the clues and try to guess the places. Put a check (✔) next to your answers. Then go to page 136 for the answers.

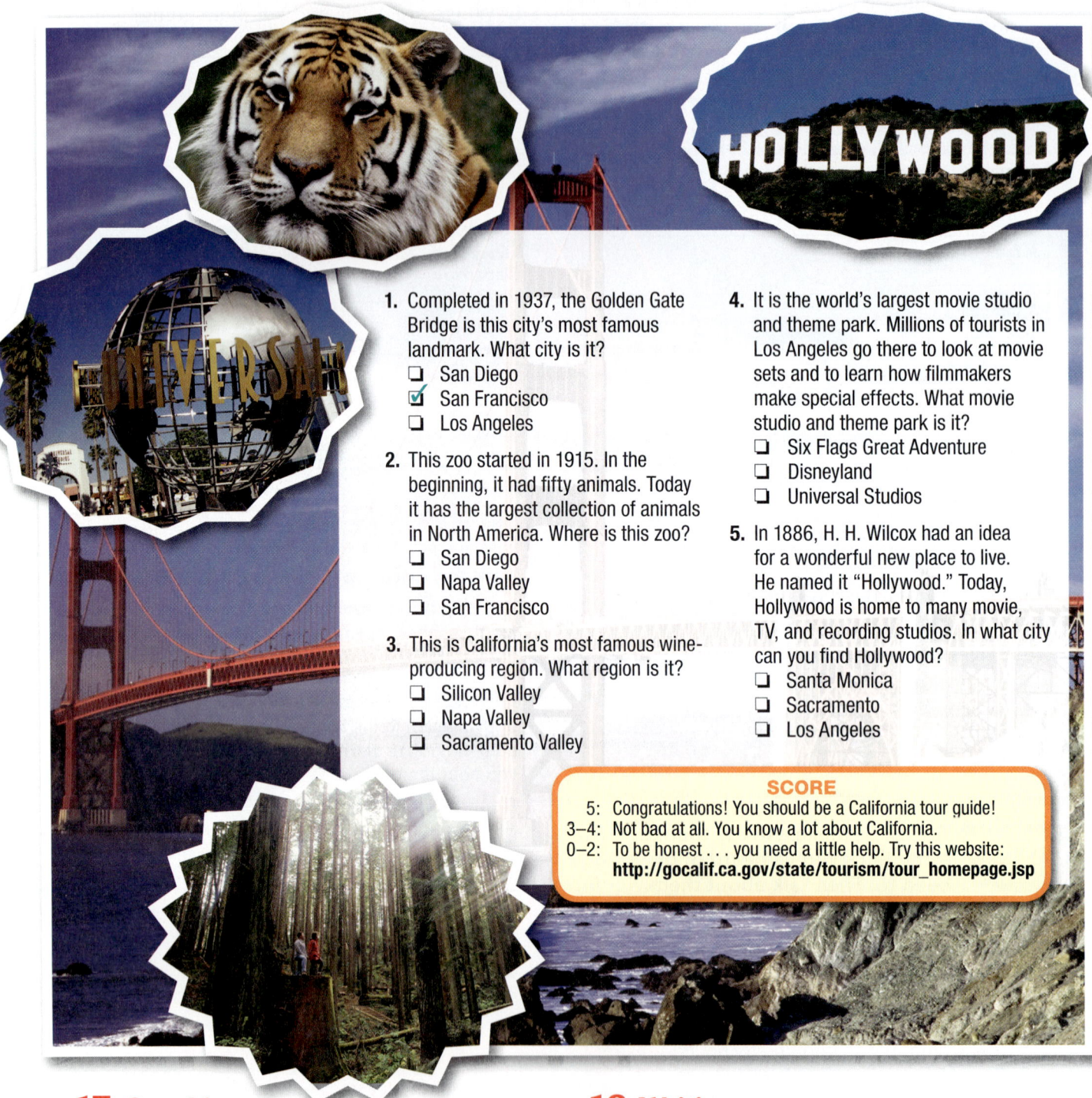

1. Completed in 1937, the Golden Gate Bridge is this city's most famous landmark. What city is it?
   - ❏ San Diego
   - ✔ San Francisco
   - ❏ Los Angeles

2. This zoo started in 1915. In the beginning, it had fifty animals. Today it has the largest collection of animals in North America. Where is this zoo?
   - ❏ San Diego
   - ❏ Napa Valley
   - ❏ San Francisco

3. This is California's most famous wine-producing region. What region is it?
   - ❏ Silicon Valley
   - ❏ Napa Valley
   - ❏ Sacramento Valley

4. It is the world's largest movie studio and theme park. Millions of tourists in Los Angeles go there to look at movie sets and to learn how filmmakers make special effects. What movie studio and theme park is it?
   - ❏ Six Flags Great Adventure
   - ❏ Disneyland
   - ❏ Universal Studios

5. In 1886, H. H. Wilcox had an idea for a wonderful new place to live. He named it "Hollywood." Today, Hollywood is home to many movie, TV, and recording studios. In what city can you find Hollywood?
   - ❏ Santa Monica
   - ❏ Sacramento
   - ❏ Los Angeles

SCORE
5: Congratulations! You should be a California tour guide!
3–4: Not bad at all. You know a lot about California.
0–2: To be honest . . . you need a little help. Try this website:
http://gocalif.ca.gov/state/tourism/tour_homepage.jsp

17 Speaking

GROUPS. Discuss these questions.

1. What are some well-known tourist places in your country? Think of at least five places.
2. What is each place famous for?
3. What can a tourist do in each place?

18 Writing

GROUPS. Write a brochure about one of the places you talked about in Exercise 17. Make your brochure appealing so that it will attract tourists. Include the sights to see and things to do there. Find or draw pictures of these things to include in your brochure.

Progress check — Units 1 and 2

> **Test-taking tip:** Start preparing for your tests early. Preparation for your first test should start right away. Review the textbook and complete your homework assignments regularly.

Grammar

A. Fill in the blanks with the simple present or the present continuous forms of the verbs. (2 points each)

1. Mom (*play*) __is playing__ the piano now. She usually (*play*) _____ at this time of the day.
2. Look. The cat (*eat*) _____ again. Believe me, this cat (*eat*) _____ all day long.
3. My neighbor (*sing*) _____ right now. Can you hear him? He always (*sing*) _____ after breakfast.
4. Charles (*work*) _____ late today. He almost never (*work*) _____ this late.
5. We (*take*) _____ French this year. Everyone (*take*) _____ a language in high school.

B. Write sentences using the present perfect or the simple past. (3 points each)

1. Nate / go for a jog on the beach / yesterday
   Nate went for a jog on the beach yesterday.
2. I / never see / a movie / about surfers
   _____
3. Ginny / ever / live / in Califonia / ?
   _____
4. Aaron / go skateboarding / yesterday / ?
   _____

C. Fill in the blanks with *the* where needed. (2 points each)

1. __The__ United States has fifty states.
2. Marcia plays _____ soccer.
3. Sometimes _____ sun hurts my eyes.
4. My favorite things are _____ books.
5. I live by _____ Pacific Ocean.
6. Why are _____ buses late today?

Vocabulary

D. Complete the sentences with the correct occupations. (2 points each)

1. A __sailor__ works on a ship.
2. An *a*_____ plays roles in movies.
3. An *e*_____ fixes other people's writing.
4. A *w*_____ writes books.
5. A *b*_____ builds things.
6. A *c*_____ leads an orchestra.

Communication

E. Complete the conversation with the sentences from the box. (2 points each)

| Not exactly. | Excuse me. |
| Sounds like a plan. | I hope so. |

A: (1) __Excuse me.__ Is this the right bus stop for the downtown bus?
B: (2) _____ I'm waiting for the downtown bus, too.
A: Do you live in this area?
B: (3) _____ I'm just visiting here. By the way, how do I get to the art museum?
A: I don't know, but I'm going there, too, so we can find it together.
B: (4) _____

> **Now I can . . .**
> ❏ make small talk.
> ❏ ask for information about transportation.
> ❏ ask for confirmation and clarification.

Game 1   *Why pie*

You need:
- a paper clip
- a pencil

Steps:

1. Divide the class into teams of two players each.

2. One member of the first team (Student 1) spins the paper clip. It will land on a slice of the pie. The player asks a "why" question using one of the phrases on that slice. The other team member (Student 2) answers the question any way he or she wants to. If they form the question and answer correctly, the team receives the number of points on that slice.

For example (the first team's paper clip has landed on the green slice):

S1: Why do you want to see a mermaid?
S2: Because it's good luck to see a mermaid.

The team receives 2 points (as indicated on the spin wheel) for forming the question and answer correctly.

3. The play continues with the next team. The first team to reach 10 points wins.

Useful language
- Your/Our turn.
- You/We win!
- The question should be . . .
- That was a good one.

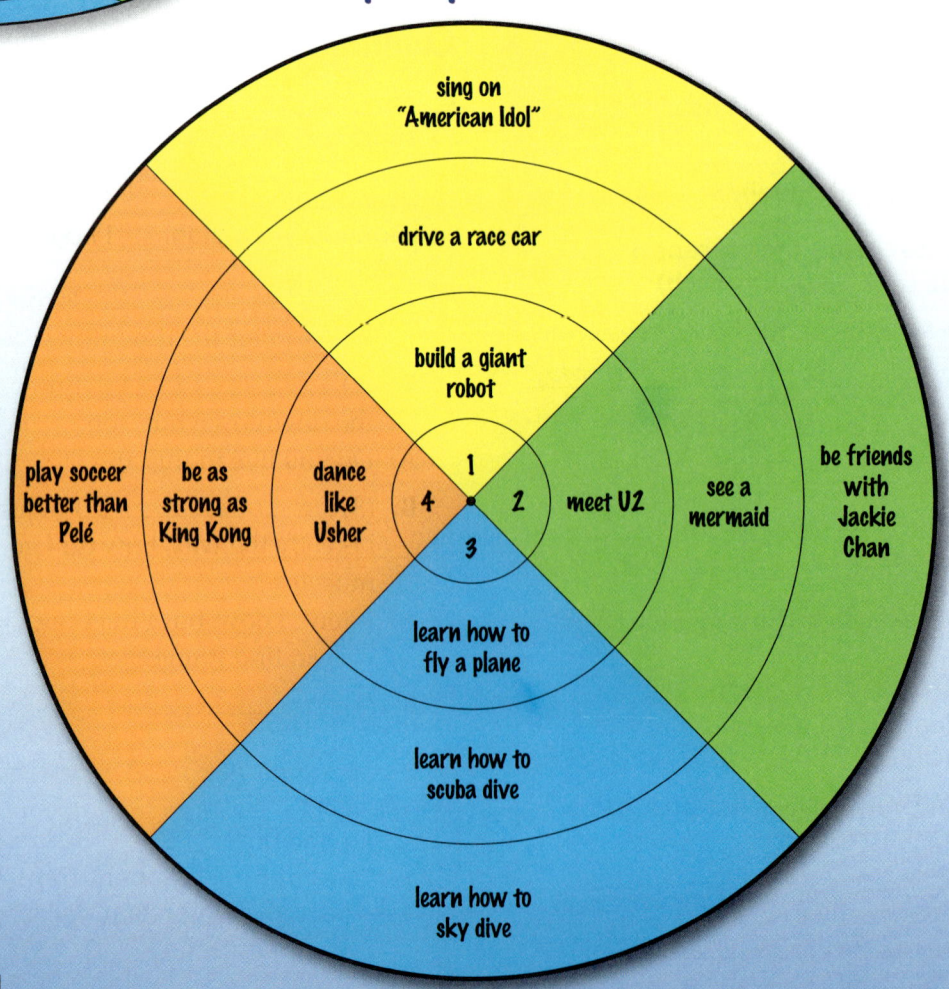

Why do you want to . . .

22   Game 1

Project 1 — A snapshot of transportation

PAIRS. Do research on a common or interesting form of transportation. It can be in your country or somewhere else in the world. Create a poster. Use the steps below as a guide. Share your poster with the class.

1. Choose the form of transportation you want to write about.

2. Discuss these questions:
   - Where do people use it?
   - What does it look like?
   - When did it first appear?
   - What is special about it?

3. Find pictures for your topics.

4. Create a mini-poster with the information and pictures that you gathered.

5. Show your poster to your classmates.

Where do people use it?

The spark sled is popular in small towns in Finland, Norway, and Sweden. People in the northern United States and Canada used the spark sled before cars.

What is special about it?

People use spark sleds for many things. In small towns you can use a spark sled as a bicycle, a wheelbarrow, a grocery cart, or even a baby stroller!

What does it look like?

A spark sled has two steel runners that cut through the snow and ice as the sled moves. And there is a wooden seat near the front of the sled.

When did it first appear?

Spark sleds first appeared in the 1800s. People used them to move easily through the snow.

Project 1   23

3 You like him, don't you?

Learning goals

Communication
Confirm information

Grammar
Should/Shouldn't; Had better/Had better not
Tag questions with *be*
Tag questions with *do*

Vocabulary
Expressions with *get*

1 Dialogue

A25 Cover the dialogue and listen.

Jack: Kelly, you really like Scott, don't you?
Kelly: Well, we get along pretty well. You don't think I'm crazy, do you? After all, I just met him.
Jack: Well, no. But I'm pretty sure this won't last.
Kelly: We'll see. Oh, Jack, could you do something for me?
Jack: It depends. It's not about Scott, is it?
Kelly: Actually, it is. Could you cover for me tomorrow?
Jack: But I'm getting together with friends.
Kelly: Please? It's just this one time.
[Phone rings]
Kelly: Hello? Oh, hi, Scott. Uh-huh. No, it's OK . . . No, I'm not upset. OK. Bye.
Jack: He canceled your date, didn't he?
Kelly: Just forget about tomorrow.
Jack: Kelly, you shouldn't let this guy get to you.
Kelly: That's easy for you to say. Oh well, I'd better get back to work.

2 Comprehension

A. Answer the questions.

1. What did Kelly ask Jack to do for her?
2. Why did Scott call Kelly?
3. Do you think Jack is a good friend?

B. **A26** Read along as you listen again. Check your answers.

24 Unit 3

3 Useful expressions

A. **A27 Listen and repeat.**
- After all
- I'm pretty sure
- It depends.
- get to (me)
- That's easy for (you) to say.

B. **Fill in the blanks. Use the expressions in Exercise A.**

1. **A:** Do you think this will last?
   B: Yeah, *I'm pretty sure* it will.
2. **A:** Isn't that noise bothering you?
   B: No. I'm not letting it _____.
3. **A:** Is it better to go by train or by bus?
   B: _____ The train is quicker, but the bus is cheaper.
4. **A:** If you try, you can finish your homework before dinner.
   B: _____ I've got a lot of homework to do.
5. **A:** I guess I should try getting a job.
   B: You should. _____, you're almost seventeen.

4 Vocabulary

Expressions with *get*

A. **A28 Listen and repeat. Then match the expressions with their meanings.**

__e__ 1. get away with something
____ 2. get together with someone
____ 3. get to someone
____ 4. get back to
____ 5. get along with someone
____ 6. get over something
____ 7. get through something

a. recover; overcome
b. complete a difficult task
c. return to
d. annoy; irritate
e. avoid punishment
f. meet; socialize
g. be friendly with

B. **Make a conversation using one of the expressions in Exercise A.**

For example:

A: I can't get over my score on that last math test. It was so bad!
B: But that was two weeks ago!
A: I know. But I can do better. I want another chance!

Unit 3   25

GRAMMAR FOCUS

**Should/Shouldn't;
Had better/Had better not**

Affirmative statements
Kelly **should** get over Scott.
Scott **had better** call again.

Negative statements
She **shouldn't** let Scott get to her.
He**'d better not** cancel again.

Note: You can use any of these phrases to give advice. Use *had better* and *had better not* to warn someone that something bad might happen if the advice isn't followed.

Discovering grammar

Look at the grammar chart. Complete the grammar rules.

1. The negative of *should* is _____.
2. The *'d* in He*'d* better is short for _____.

Practicing grammar

5 Practice

Match the statements with the responses. Write the letter in the blanks.

__d__ 1. I don't know what to wear.
____ 2. Dad's asleep.
____ 3. John is really hurt. His arm might be broken.
____ 4. I think it's a little cold in here.
____ 5. They're not ready for the final exam.

a. We'd better go find the coach.
b. They'd better stay home and study this weekend.
c. You'd better not wake him up.
d. You should wear your jeans.
e. You should close the window.

6 Practice

Give advice with *should, shouldn't, had better,* or *had better not*. Use phrases from the box in your responses.

get ready for school	get together
get away with it	go to bed late
call home	study harder

1. **A:** Bill failed another one of his tests.
   B: I know. (*had better*)
   He'd better study harder next time.

2. **A:** Oh, no! We missed the bus!
   B: Mom will be worried. (*should*)
   _____

3. **A:** I heard Lenny cheated on the final exam.
   B: That's not fair to us. (*had better not*)
   _____

4. **A:** I feel tired every morning.
   B: Really? (*shouldn't*)
   _____

5. **A:** I miss hanging out with you.
   B: Same here. (*should*)
   _____

6. **A:** Mom, what time is it?
   B: It's already seven o'clock. (*had better*)
   _____

7 Listening

A29 Listen to the conversation. Then answer the questions.

1. What advice does Aunt Paula give to Kelly?
2. What does Kelly decide she should do?
3. Do you think Kelly understood Aunt Paula's advice?

GROUPS. Talk about who you go to for advice.

Useful language:
- Who do you talk to when you have a problem?
- I go to (my mother) for advice.
- (My friends) give me the best advice.
- I don't talk to anyone.

GRAMMAR FOCUS

Tag questions with *be*

Affirmative statements	Negative tags	Expected answers
Jack **is working** today,	**isn't** he?	**Yes**, he **is**.
The boys **are** great,	**aren't** they?	**Yes**, they **are**.
The party **was** fun,	**wasn't** it?	**Yes**, it **was**.
They **were** just here,	**weren't** they?	**Yes**, they **were**.

Negative statements	Affirmative tags	Expected answers
Kelly **isn't** upset,	**is** she?	**No**, she **isn't**.
They **aren't listening**,	**are** they?	**No**, they **aren't**.
He **wasn't** jealous,	**was** he?	**No**, he **wasn't**.
They **weren't sleeping**,	**were** they?	**No**, they **weren't**.

Discovering grammar

Look at the grammar chart. Complete the grammar rules.

(**1.**) A tag question is a ___statement___ followed by a short _____ at the end. (**2.**) When the verb in the statement is affirmative, the tag question is _____. (**3.**) When the verb in the statement is negative, the tag question is _____.

Practicing grammar

8 Practice

Circle the correct endings to the tag questions.

1. You were nervous during your speech, (*were you* / *weren't you*)?
2. You're all in 9th grade, (*are you* / *aren't you*)?
3. Charlie's not here yet, (*is he* / *isn't he*)?
4. They weren't here, (*were they* / *weren't they*)?
5. They're finished with their project, (*are they* / *aren't they*)?
6. This isn't difficult, (*is it* / *isn't it*)?

9 Practice

Add tags to complete the questions. Then write the expected answers.

1. **A:** You weren't looking for me, ___were you___?
   B: ___No, I wasn't.___
2. **A:** She was looking forward to the show, _____?
   B: _____
3. **A:** They aren't looking out the window, _____?
   B: _____
4. **A:** The teachers were looking over the test scores, _____?
   B: _____
5. **A:** He's looking up at the stars, _____?
   B: _____

10 Practice

Have a competition! Go to page 130.

Unit 3 27

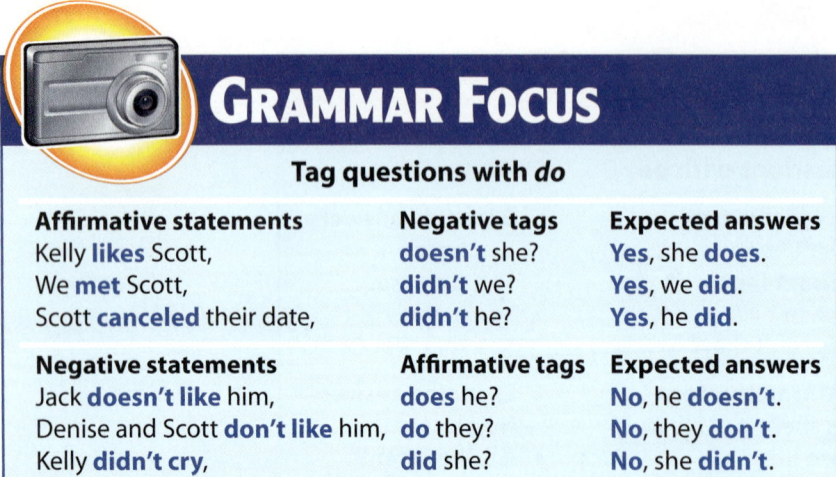

GRAMMAR FOCUS

Tag questions with *do*

Affirmative statements	Negative tags	Expected answers
Kelly **likes** Scott,	**doesn't** she?	**Yes**, she **does**.
We **met** Scott,	**didn't** we?	**Yes**, we **did**.
Scott **canceled** their date,	**didn't** he?	**Yes**, he **did**.

Negative statements	Affirmative tags	Expected answers
Jack **doesn't like** him,	**does** he?	**No**, he **doesn't**.
Denise and Scott **don't like** him,	**do** they?	**No**, they **don't**.
Kelly **didn't cry**,	**did** she?	**No**, she **didn't**.

Discovering grammar

Look at the grammar chart. Match the tag question with the expected answer to show you understand the rules. Write the letter on the line.

_____ 1. She likes him, doesn't she?   a. No, she doesn't.
_____ 2. She doesn't like him, does she?   b. No, she didn't.
_____ 3. She liked him, didn't she?   c. Yes, she does.
_____ 4. She didn't like him, did she?   d. Yes, she did.

Practicing grammar

11 Practice

Circle the correct endings to the tag questions.

1. The students get along well, (*do they* / *(don't they)*)?
2. It rains a lot in Costa Rica, (*does it* / *doesn't it*)?
3. Sara doesn't visit often, (*does she* / *doesn't she*)?
4. He missed his bus, (*did he* / *didn't he*)?
5. Mark doesn't call you every day, (*does he* / *doesn't he*)?
6. You didn't do your homework, (*did you* / *didn't you*)?

12 Practice

Add tags to complete the questions. Then write the expected answers.

1. A: You and your sister take turns driving, _____?
   B: Yes, we do.

2. A: The plane took off at noon, _____?
   B: _____

3. A: They didn't take down my posters, _____?
   B: _____

4. A: You don't want to walk my dog while I'm away, _____?
   B: _____

5. A: He took her out to dinner last night, _____?
   B: _____

13 Your turn

A. Write two questions you think you know the answer to but aren't sure about. Write them on strips of paper and give them to your teacher. Use tags in your questions.

1. Brazil beat Germany in the 2002 World Cup, didn't they?
2. Our teacher's birthday is May 20th, isn't it?

B. **CLASS.** Your teacher will read some of the questions aloud. Maybe your question will be answered!

28   Unit 3

14 Practice

Read the conversation. Complete the tag questions.

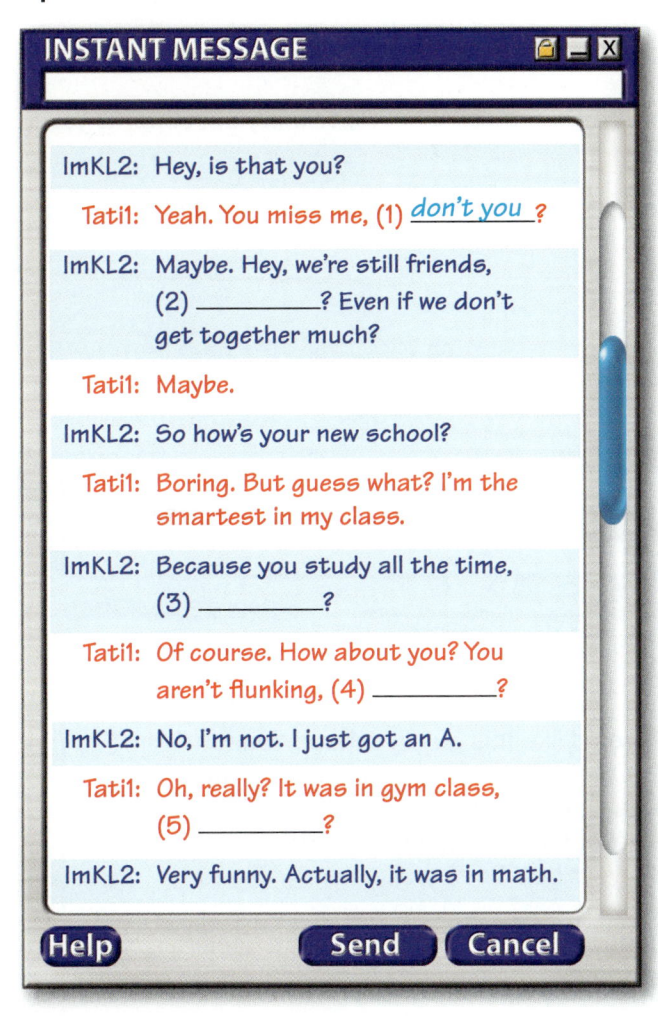

INSTANT MESSAGE

ImKL2: Hey, is that you?

Tati1: Yeah. You miss me, (1) *don't you*?

ImKL2: Maybe. Hey, we're still friends, (2) _____? Even if we don't get together much?

Tati1: Maybe.

ImKL2: So how's your new school?

Tati1: Boring. But guess what? I'm the smartest in my class.

ImKL2: Because you study all the time, (3) _____?

Tati1: Of course. How about you? You aren't flunking, (4) _____?

ImKL2: No, I'm not. I just got an A.

Tati1: Oh, really? It was in gym class, (5) _____?

ImKL2: Very funny. Actually, it was in math.

15 Pronunciation

Intonation patterns in tag questions

A. **A30** Listen and repeat.

Not sure (rising intonation)

You like him, don't you?   He's here, isn't he?

Sure (falling intonation)

You like him, don't you?   He's here, isn't he?

B. **A31** Listen to the conversation in Exercise 14. Circle the intonation pattern you hear for each tag.

1. Rising   (Falling)
2. Rising   Falling
3. Rising   Falling
4. Rising   Falling
5. Rising   Falling

C. **PAIRS.** Read the conversation in Exercise 14 aloud. Use proper intonation for the tag questions.

16 Communication

Confirm information

A. **A32** Listen and read.

A: Excuse me. You live near here, don't you?
B: Yes, I do. Wait . . . you're Susan's little brother, aren't you?
A: Yes, I am.
B: I used to baby-sit you! You don't remember me, do you?
A: Umm . . . I'm not sure.
B: I used to make you peanut butter, honey, and banana sandwiches all the time. Remember?
A: Oh, yeah! Now I remember you!

B. **PAIRS.** Write a conversation similar to the one in Exercise A. It should be about two people who haven't seen each other in a long time. Use tag questions like *don't you?* or *aren't you?*

C. **GROUPS.** Role-play your conversation in front of another pair.

Unit 3   29

Learn to learn

Skim for the main idea.

To *skim* means to read very quickly. After you skim a reading, you will have a general idea of what the reading is about. Then when you read the selection again (more carefully, this time), you will have better comprehension.

A. You have 30 seconds. Skim Cindy's e-mail in Exercise 17. Don't stop for details or worry about words you don't understand.

B. **PAIRS.** What's the general idea of Cindy's e-mail? Discuss this with your classmate. Then go on to Exercise 17.

17 Reading

A33 Read along as you listen to Cindy's e-mail.

To: Mark
CC:
Subject: What do u think?

Hey, Mark,

What's up? Listen, I need your opinion. You see, I like this guy in school. You're probably laughing right now, aren't you? It's OK. You can laugh. Just answer me honestly. You remember Josh from the Drama Club, don't you? Tall, dark-haired, blue eyes? Last year's best actor? Well, he never talked to me before. He probably didn't even know I existed. But this year he's been really friendly. He started to pay attention to me after we talked at a cast party. Now, every time he sees me, he comes over to talk or to walk me to my class. But that's all he does. He hasn't asked for my phone number, so of course, he never calls me.

Can I call him? I really, really like him. Do you think he likes me, too? Should I give him my phone number? What do guys think when a girl shows a guy that she likes him? What do you think I should do?

Cindy

18 Comprehension

Answer the questions.

1. What's the main reason for Cindy's e-mail?
2. What does Josh do when he sees Cindy?
3. What kind of friendship do you think Cindy and Mark have? Explain your answer.

19 Writing

A. Pretend that you are Cindy's friend. Respond to her e-mail. Write your e-mail in your notebook.

B. **PAIRS.** Read your classmate's e-mail. Did you give similar advice?

Putting it together *A bad start*

A. **A34** Read along as you listen. What does Jack's little brother want to do?

1.
- Hi, Kelly. What's the matter? It's not about Scott, is it?
- Well . . .

2.
- Are you OK? Would you rather be alone?
- No, stay. It's just that Scott canceled our date.
- You're kidding! Did he give you a reason?

3.
- Kind of. I'm not sure if it's the truth. . . . Hi, Jack.
- Ooh! Those look good, don't they?
- I made this one especially for you, Kelly.

4.
- Jack! It's time to — Wow! Who's that?
- Who? Oh, you mean Denise? She's pretty, isn't she? What are you doing here?
- We're picking you up. Mom's outside.

5.
- Denise, Kelly, this is my brother, Matt.
- I'm almost 12.
- Hi, Matt. You're cute! How old are you?

6.
- Can I stay with you for the afternoon? Please?
- It's OK, Jack. Matt can hang out with us.
- You're lucky I have such nice friends. Yes, you can stay. But first, you should ask Mom if we can stay longer.

B. **GROUPS.** Discuss this question: What advice would you give to Kelly about Scott?

Unit 3   31

Wide Angle on the world

1 Reading

> **Reading skill:** Scanning
> When you scan an article, you read very quickly and look only for the information you need.

Scan the article "Surfing: Hawaiian Style" and look for the answers to the following questions.

1. The qualities required in a surfer and a leader:
   ____courage____ and _____
2. The nickname of Duke Kahanamoku, Hawaii's most famous surfer: _____
3. Three popular surfer expressions:
   _____, _____, and _____

2 Speaking

GROUPS. Read the article again. Then discuss the following questions.

1. Why do you think surfing was popular with kings and queens?
2. Is surfing cool? What do you like about surfing culture?

3 Listening

A35 Listen to the report. Then circle the letter of the correct answer.

1. What is the first rule of surfing?
   a. You must be able to dive.   (b.) You must be able to swim well.
2. When bodysurfing, what should you do first?
   a. get in the water and try it   b. study the waves
3. Which board has a cord attached to the surfer's wrist?
   a. a bodyboard   b. a surfboard
4. What is angling?
   a. moving a board on a wave   b. standing on a board

4 Writing

In your notebook, write about a sport that is popular in your country. Explain its beginnings and the skills needed to play or do it.

32   Wide Angle 1

Surfing: HAWAIIAN Style

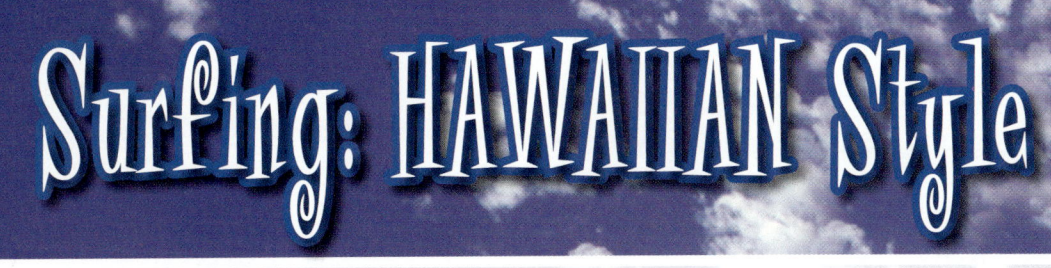

Spectacular! Awesome! Amazing! These are words often used to describe a surfer riding a 15- to 20-foot wave. Competitive surfers need courage and strength, the same qualities needed by great leaders. It is not surprising that in old Hawaii surfing was a sport for kings and queens.

When the first Europeans visited the Hawaiian islands in the 1700s, surfing was a popular sport. Later, in the early 1900s, Hawaii's most beloved surfer appeared on the scene. His name was Duke Kahanamoku, but sports fans called him the "Human Fish." Duke was very daring. According to Hawaiian legend, Duke once surfed huge waves that resulted from a Japanese earthquake. Duke also gave surfing demonstrations to inspire others to try the sport.

Bethany Hamilton is another Hawaiian surfer who is well known for courage and strength. At the age of 13, Bethany was surfing when a shark attacked her and bit off her arm. But that didn't stop Bethany. Soon after her injury, she jumped back on her surfboard. Now Bethany's a world-class competitor who has also written a book about her sport. She hopes the book will inspire other girls to surf. As surfers would say, she's "totally righteous!"

Today, surfing is the hippest of sports. Surfers are considered cool, and surfer fashions such as hooded sweatshirts, long, baggy shorts, flip-flops, and T-shirts are popular among teens. Surfer slang terms such as *dude* (man), *stoked* (enthusiastic), and *chill* (calm down) have found their way into everyday language. Clearly, surfing has become more than an international sport. It's also a lifestyle.

Wide Angle 1

4 I've been sitting here...

1 Dialogue

A36 Cover the dialogue and listen.

Guest 1: Excuse me, miss. I've been waiting for my order for half an hour. Is it ready yet?

Kelly: No, not yet.

Guest 1: Never mind. Just cancel my order!

Guest 2: Excuse me! I've been sitting here for a while now. All I want is coffee.

Kelly: Oh. You should have told me that sooner.

Aunt Paula: Kelly, can I have a word with you? I've been watching you all morning. I'm not happy with the way you've been treating our guests.

Kelly: But Aunt Paula, you heard the way they talked to me.

Aunt Paula: Hold it right there, Kelly. Our guests expect politeness and patience from us.

Kelly: I'm sorry. You're right. I should have been nicer to them.

Learning goals

Communication
Express regret

Grammar
The present perfect and the present perfect continuous
Should have/Shouldn't have

Vocabulary
Adjective to noun transformation

2 Comprehension

A. Answer the questions.

1. Why are the guests upset?
2. Why does Aunt Paula scold Kelly?
3. What excuse does Kelly give for her behavior?

B. **A37** Read along as you listen again. Check your answers.

3 Useful expressions

A. **A38** Listen and repeat.

- Never mind.
- All I want is (coffee).
- Can I have a word with you?
- Hold it right there.

B. **PAIRS.** Which expressions from Exercise A would be appropriate to say for these situations?

1. You're a parent. You need to talk to your child about something he/she did wrong.
   Can I have a word with you?

2. Your friend says something about you that isn't true. You're upset, and you want her to stop talking so you can correct her.
   _____

3. You've told your friend something three times. He asks you to repeat it again. You decide it's not worth the trouble.
   _____

4. Your dad asks what you want for your birthday. Your only wish is for a really good pair of running shoes.
   _____

4 Vocabulary

Adjective to noun transformation

A. Look at some of the ways adjectives are transformed into nouns.

+ -ce	+ -ness
patient → patien**ce**	polite → polite**ness**
+ -y	+ -ity
honest → honest**y**	humble → humil**ity**

B. With the help of a dictionary, change the adjectives below into nouns.

1. kind _____*kindness*_____
2. generous _____
3. nervous _____
4. difficult _____
5. silent _____
6. popular _____
7. jealous _____
8. confident _____

C. Underline the adjectives in the sentences below. Then form nouns from the underlined adjectives and rewrite the sentences.

1. Kelly is impatient. This upsets the guests.
   Kelly's impatience upsets the guests.

2. Jack is polite. This impresses the guests.
   _____

3. Jack stayed silent. This upset Kelly.
   _____

4. The inn is popular. This is because of the food they serve there.
   _____
   _____

5. Aunt Paula is unhappy. This is because of Kelly's behavior.
   _____
   _____

Unit 4   35

GRAMMAR FOCUS

The present perfect and the present perfect continuous

Present perfect
Denise **has called** Kelly three times today.
Denise and Kelly **have walked** together on the beach several times.

Present perfect continuous
Denise **has been talking** to Kelly for an hour now.
Denise and Kelly **have been walking** on the beach since 10:00.

Discovering grammar

Look at the grammar chart. Complete the grammar rules by writing *PP* (for the present perfect) or *PPC* (for the present perfect continuous) in the blanks.

1. __PPC__ is used for a repeated actions in the past that have a connection to the present.

2. _____ is used for a completed action that began sometime in the past and has a connection to the present.

3. _____ is used for an action that began sometime in the past, has a connection to the present, and is unfinished or temporary.

Practicing grammar

5 Practice

Complete the sentences with the present perfect or the present perfect continuous form of the verbs in parentheses.

1. Kelly (*work*) __has worked__ at the inn before.
   She (*work*) __has been working__ at the inn for three weeks.

2. Scott (*compete*) _____ in surfing events in the past. He (*compete*) _____ in them since he was young.

3. Jack and Denise (*plan*) _____ a trip to Universal Studios. They (*plan*) _____ it for a few weeks.

6 Practice

Complete the sentences with the present perfect or the present perfect continuous form of the verbs in parentheses. You may use contractions.

1. Jill (*be*) __'s been__ on safari twice. How cool is that?

2. I (*eat*) _____ dinner at their house many times. Mrs. Hill's a great cook.

3. You're still reading that book? You (*read*) _____ it for months!

4. We (*shop*) _____ for three hours now.

5. You (*work*) _____ on the computer all day. Take a break!

6. Of course, I (*see*) _____ *Harry Potter and the Goblet of Fire*. In fact, I (*see*) _____ all the Harry Potter movies twice.

7 Practice

A. Answer the questions. Use your own information.

1. How long have you been studying English?
   I've been studying English for (eight) years now.

2. What books have you read in English?
   _____

3. What have you done more than once today?
   _____

4. What have you never done before, but would like to try?
   _____

5. What have you been doing recently?
   _____

B. **PAIRS.** Take turns asking and answering the questions in Exercise A.

8 Practice

Have a competition! Go page 131.

36 Unit 4

9 Listening

A39 Listen to the news report. Circle the correct answers.

1. Sabrina is in ____.
   a. college
   b. middle school
   c. high school

2. She has been studying how to fight ____ since her freshman year.
   a. drug use
   b. cybercrime
   c. street crime

3. An example she gives of cybercrime is ____.
   a. identity theft
   b. viruses
   c. bank fraud

4. She has also been learning how ____ operate.
   a. video games
   b. police cars
   c. hackers

5. She has been ____ in her free time.
   a. hacking computers
   b. building a computer
   c. playing video games

10 Writing

A. Read the e-mail below.

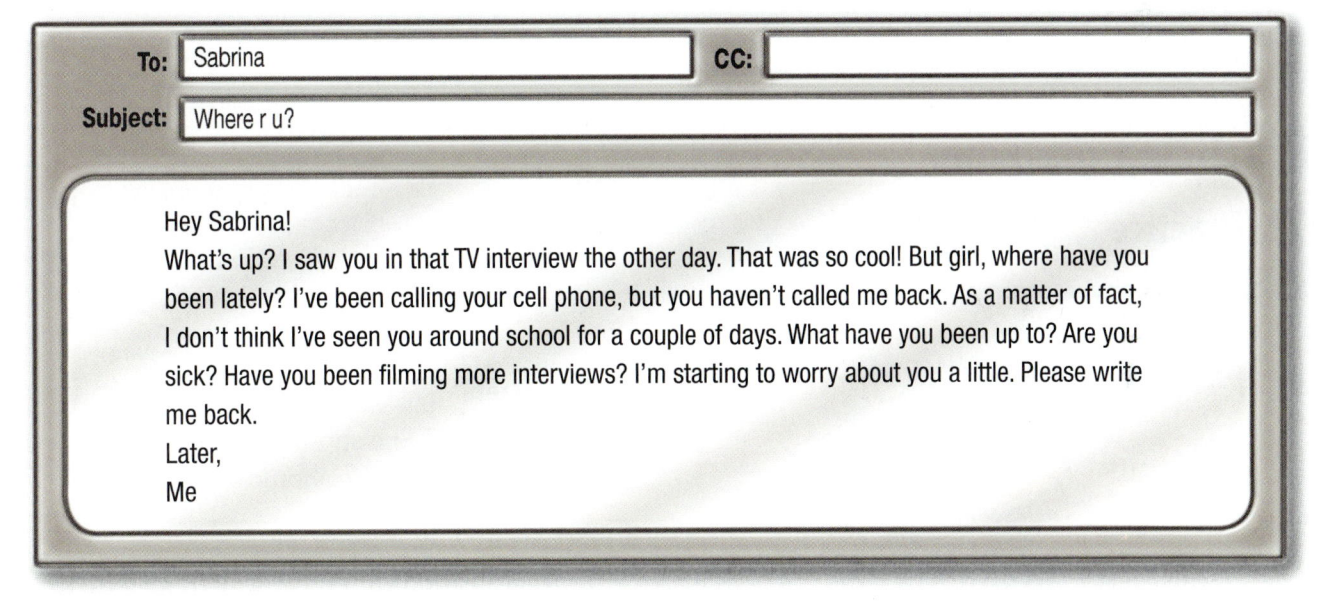

To: Sabrina
CC:
Subject: Where r u?

Hey Sabrina!
What's up? I saw you in that TV interview the other day. That was so cool! But girl, where have you been lately? I've been calling your cell phone, but you haven't called me back. As a matter of fact, I don't think I've seen you around school for a couple of days. What have you been up to? Are you sick? Have you been filming more interviews? I'm starting to worry about you a little. Please write me back.
Later,
Me

B. Write a reply to the e-mail in Exercise A in your notebook. Write it as if from Sabrina. Use the present perfect and the present perfect continuous.

TEEN TALK

GROUPS. Talk about something you've been thinking about doing. Describe what you've done so far (if anything) to make it happen.

Useful language:
- I've been thinking about getting a new . . .
- I've been talking with my parents about starting a . . .
- I've started getting information online about . . .

Unit 4   37

GRAMMAR FOCUS

Should have/Shouldn't have

Kelly **should have been** polite to the guests.
She **should have asked** Jack for help.
She **shouldn't have been** rude.
She **shouldn't have treated** the guests badly.

Discovering grammar

Look at the grammar chart. Choose the correct answer. Write the letter in the blanks.

1. *Should have* and *shouldn't have* must be followed by the _____ participle form of the main verb.
   a. present   b. past

2. Use *should have* and *shouldn't have* to express advice, regret, and criticism about _____ situations.
   a. present   b. past

Practicing grammar

11 Practice

A. Read the conversation.

Sam: Hey Don! Mike and JJ just called from the concert. Mike said we should have gone with them because someone gave them extra tickets!
Don: Really? Let's go!
Sam: Wait. Don't you need to ask your parents for permission?
Don: They're not home yet.
Sam: Maybe you should call them, or at least leave a note.
Don: I'll call them from the concert. I'll take my dad's cell phone. Uh-oh.... Where's my jacket? I'll just use my brother's.
Sam: Shouldn't you ask them first?
Don: My dad won't mind, and my brother won't even know I used his jacket.

B. PAIRS. Write pairs of sentences. Say what Don shouldn't and should have done.

1. Don shouldn't have gone out while his parents were away.
   Don should have called his parents to ask for permission to go to the concert.

2. _____

3. _____

12 Pronunciation

Reduced forms: *should have* and *shouldn't have*

A. 🔊 **A40 Listen.**

should have / She should have stayed.
shouldn't have / She shouldn't have left.

B. 🔊 **A41 Listen and repeat.**

1. A: You shouldn't have waited so long to call me.
   B: I know. I should have called you sooner.
2. A: You should have seen that show on TV last night. It was great!
   B: Oh, man. I shouldn't have gone to bed so early.

C. PAIRS. Practice the conversations in Exercise B.

38   Unit 4

13 Reading

A42 Read along as you listen to Pam's letter to Ms. Manners.

Dear Ms. Manners:

I recently went to Japan with my parents. We stayed in the house of my father's business associate. Our first day there was embarrassing. When we got to the house, I started to walk into the living room with my shoes on. Then suddenly, I remembered—I was supposed to take off my shoes!

At dinnertime, we were using chopsticks to eat. I stuck my chopsticks in my rice while I drank some water. Then I noticed Mrs. Kamaguchi looking at them with a strange look on her face. I casually took the chopsticks out of the rice and put them next to my plate. Later I found out you shouldn't stick chopsticks into rice (or any other food) because this is only done at funerals.

After dinner, my mother and I helped clear the table and brought the dirty dishes to the kitchen. Mrs. Kamaguchi looked embarrassed and apologized to us. I thought we were being polite, but in Japan, guests aren't supposed to help clean up.

The next day, we bought a book on Japanese culture, which we should have done earlier. The rest of our visit went much better.

I hope you share this experience with your readers so they can learn from our mistakes.

Sincerely,
Pam

14 Comprehension

Look at the reading in Exercise 13. What are three mistakes Pam made on her visit to Japan?

1. _She shouldn't have . . ._
2. _____
3. _____

15 Communication

Express regret

A. **A43** Listen and read.

   A: So how was your trip to the United States?
   B: It was great. I made some embarrassing mistakes though.
   A: Like?
   B: Well, I was waiting for the bus one day, and when it arrived, I rushed to get on. I shouldn't have done that.
   A: Why not?
   B: I should have waited until the people in front of me got on the bus.
   A: Really? That's interesting.

B. **PAIRS.** Imagine you visited Japan recently. Write a conversation similar to the one in Exercise A. Use the information in Pam's letter in Exercise 13.

16 Your turn

A. **GROUPS.** Make a list of any rules or customs you know or have heard about in other cultures.

   For example:

   Place: many Spanish
   speaking countries
   Custom: Girls have a big
   party when they turn 15
   years old.

B. **CLASS.** Discuss your completed lists with your classmates.

Unit 4 39

17 Speaking

A. GROUPS. Read the situations below. Discuss your answers to the questions. When you have finished, turn to page 136 to check your answers.

What Should You Have Done?

1. You were an exchange student in the United States. You were staying with an American family. It was your birthday. Your host family gave you a present wrapped in colorful paper. You thanked them for the present, but they were still standing in front of you, waiting. What should you have done or said?

2. You invited a Korean friend over to your house. Your mom thought she had very nice hair. The next day you told your friend what your mom said. Your friend denied the compliment and said, "No, it's not." Should you have given your friend this compliment?

3. You were in a restaurant in Morocco with your parents. Your food arrived on one big platter. You noticed a big bowl of water next to your plate, but you didn't have any utensils. Should you have asked for utensils?

4. You were visiting a Russian friend's home. You saw a beautiful doll on a table. You told your friend that you thought the doll was beautiful. Should you have told her this?

B. GROUPS. Compare the customs you just read about with the corresponding customs in your country.

Learn to learn

Understand other cultures.

When you meet people from other countries, make an effort to understand their cultures.

A. Think about how you relate to people from other cultures. Put a check (✔) next to the items that apply:

- ❏ When new students come to my school from other countries, I try to make friends with them.
- ❏ I like to learn about other cultures by asking people questions.
- ❏ I like to learn about other cultures by reading books, magazines, and online articles.
- ❏ I enjoy the differences between my culture and others. I think the differences are interesting.

B. Look at the things you checked. Continue to develop these. Now, look at what you didn't check. Think of ways you can improve how you learn about other cultures.

40 Unit 4

Progress check Units 3 and 4

> **Test-taking tip:** Join a study group.
> You can test your understanding by asking and answering questions with your classmates.

Grammar

A. Rewrite the sentences. Use the present perfect continuous and the cues. (3 points each)

1. It started to rain this morning. It's evening, and it is still raining. (*all day*)
   It has been raining all day.

2. He started to study at 8:00 P.M. It is now 11:00 P.M., and he is still studying. (*for*)
   _____

3. Rob tried to reach you on the phone this morning. It's evening, and he is still trying to reach you. (*all day*)
   _____

4. My teacher and my mom started talking at 10 o'clock. They are still talking. (*since*)
   _____

5. Jessie started jogging at 6:00 A.M. It is now 8:00 A.M., and she is still jogging. (*for*)
   _____

B. Write responses based on the cues. Use *had better* or *had better not*. (4 points each)

1. **A:** I should have remembered mom's birthday.
   B: *I know. You'd better not forget it* next year.

2. **A:** Laura shouldn't have been so rude to Mark.
   B: _____ again.

3. **A:** Theo should have offered to pay for his lunch.
   B: _____ next time.

4. **A:** Cecelia shouldn't have brought her little brother to the party.
   B: _____ again.

Vocabulary

C. Write the noun forms of these adjectives. (2 points each)

1. difficult *difficulty*
2. kind _____
3. patient _____
4. polite _____
5. nervous _____
6. popular _____
7. generous _____
8. honest _____

D. Complete the sentences with words from the box. (2 points each)

| get along | get over |
| get through | get together |

1. Let's _____ after school to study.
2. Jessica can't _____ her old boyfriend. She still thinks about him.
3. My dog and my cat _____ really well. They're like best friends.
4. My friends always help me _____ tough times.

Communication

E. PAIRS. In your notebook, write a conversation about the situation below. Then read it aloud. (4 points)

The clerk at the market is someone you know. You haven't seen him or her for a long time. You used to be on the same soccer team. Use tag questions to confirm information.

Now I can...
❏ make my advice sound stronger.
❏ confirm information.
❏ express regret.

5 The bigger the waves,...

1 Dialogue

A44 Cover the dialogue and listen.

Denise: Hi, Scott.
Scott: Hi, guys! What are you doing here? Did you come to watch me surf?
Kelly: No, not really.
Scott: Sure you did. Oh, this is Kenji.
Denise: Hi, Kenji.
Kenji: Hi.
Scott: Kenji's from Japan. We surfed together yesterday.
Kenji: The waves were much smaller than they are today.
Scott: Yeah. That's why I didn't do so well yesterday.
Kelly: You surfed badly and blame the waves?
Scott: Sure I do. The bigger the waves, the better the surfing. The waves are a lot bigger today.
Kenji: They're far more challenging, that's for sure.
Kelly: I don't know, Scott. Maybe the problem was your surfing and not the waves.
Denise: Kelly, give Scott a break. Let's see if he can do better this time. Go ahead, Scott.
Scott: Let's get going, Kenji. We'll show them how we ride the waves.
Denise: Catch you later.

Learning goals

Communication
Make comparisons

Grammar
Comparative and superlative forms of adverbs
Comparatives with *a lot*, *far*, and *much*
Double comparatives: *the . . . the*

Vocabulary
Word building

2 Comprehension

A. Read the sentences. Cross out the wrong information. Then correct the sentences.

1. Kelly is feeling ~~friendly~~ *unfriendly* toward Scott.
2. Scott and Kenji jogged together yesterday.
3. Yesterday the waves were bigger than they are today.
4. Scott blames his bad surfing on himself.
5. Denise thinks Kelly is being fair to Scott.

B. A45 Read along as you listen again. Check your answers.

3 Useful expressions

A. A46 Listen and repeat.
- Sure I do. / Sure you did.
- Give (me) a break.
- Go ahead.
- Let's get going.
- Catch you later.

B. Complete the conversation with the expressions in Exercise A.

Ted: Do you want to surf?
Ross: *Sure I do.* _____
Ted: OK. But wait while I say goodbye to Sandy.
Ross: Sure. _____

Ted: Bye, Sandy. _____
Sandy: Bye! Don't be gone too long!
Ted: I won't.

Ted: OK, Ross. _____
Ross: About time! It's already four o'clock.
Ted: _____ I had to say goodbye to Sandy.

C. GROUPS. Write a short conversation similar to the one in Exercise B. Role-play your conversation in front of another group.

Unit 5 43

GRAMMAR FOCUS

Comparative and superlative forms of adverbs

One-syllable adverbs	Comparative form	Superlative form
fast	fast**er** than	the fast**est**
late	lat**er** than	the lat**est**
Adverbs ending in -ly	**Comparative form**	**Superlative form**
quickly	**more** quickly **than**	the **most** quickly
Irregular adverbs	**Comparative form**	**Superlative form**
well	**better than**	the **best**
badly	**worse than**	the **worst**
far	**farther/further than**	the **farthest/furthest**

Discovering grammar

Look at the grammar chart. Complete the grammar rules.

1. For one-syllable adverbs add ___-er___ to make the comparative and _____ to make the superlative.
2. If an adverb ends in -ly use _____ to make the comparative and _____ to make the superlative.

Practicing grammar

4 Practice

Fill in the blanks with the comparative and superlative forms of the adverbs in bold.

1. Jeff ran pretty **fast** today. But Kevin ran ___faster than___ Jeff. Matt ran ___the fastest___ of the three.
2. Kimiko arrived **late** to class. Aiko arrived _____ Kimiko. And Michi arrived _____ of all.
3. Ali plays soccer **well**. He plays _____ Carlos. He's _____ of anyone on the team.
4. Richie sings quite **badly**. But Al sings _____ Richie. Louisa sings _____ of all.
5. Luis writes **carefully**. I write _____ Luis. Janet writes _____ of all.

5 Practice

PAIRS. Look at the chart. Compare the runners. Answer the questions with complete sentences.

	Date	Bonnie	Alice	Jackie
800 M Run	4/27/06	2:10.05	2:13.43	2:10.35
	5/31/06	2:15.30	2:16.18	2:14.98*
3000 M Run	4/27/06	n/a	10:13.51	10:06.10
	5/31/06	10:36.14	10:40.46	10:31.00*
400 M Low Hurdle	4/27/06	1:10.52	1:03.10*	n/a
	5/31/06	1:06.71	1:10.38	n/a

*indicates state title won

1. Who ran 800 meters the fastest?
2. Who did better overall in the long distance runs?
3. Who won the most state titles?
4. Ask your own question about the chart.

6 Practice

Have a competition! Go to page 131.

44 Unit 5

GRAMMAR FOCUS

Comparatives with *a lot*, *far*, and *much*

Adjectives	Adverbs
Hawaii is **(a lot) warmer** than Alaska.	Denise greeted Scott **(a lot) more warmly** than Kelly.
Kenji is a **(far) more powerful** surfer than Scott.	Kenji surfs **(far) more powerfully** than Scott.
Kenji's moves are **(much) more daring** than Scott's.	Kenji moves **(much) more daringly** than Scott.

Discovering grammar

Look at the grammar chart. Circle the correct answers.

1. The phrases *a lot warmer*, *far warmer*, and *much warmer* have _____ .
   a. about the same meaning
   b. very different meanings
2. *A lot*, *far*, and *much* before a comparative make the comparative _____.
   a. stronger   b. weaker

Practicing grammar

7 Practice

Compare and combine the phrases below. Make the comparisons stronger by adding *a lot*, *far*, or *much*.

1. Harry Potter movies / Harry Potter books
   interesting (*much*)
   The Harry Potter books are much more
   interesting than the Harry Potter movies.

2. rap music / classical music
   popular (*far*)
   _____
   _____

3. playing sports / watching sports on TV
   fun (*a lot*)
   _____
   _____

4. adults / young people
   play their music loudly (*much*)
   _____
   _____

5. girls I know / boys I know
   draw well (*a lot*)
   _____
   _____

8 Pronunciation

Use intonation for emphasis

A. **A47** Listen to the sentences. Underline the words that are stressed for emphasis.

1. Tim kicks a soccer ball a lot harder than Ed.
2. Lisa throws a ball far better than Sam.
3. Ken swims much more powerfully than Mia.
4. Pablo is a far better diver than Pete.

B. **PAIRS.** Review each other's answers. Then take turns reading the sentences aloud.

TEEN TALK

GROUPS. Compare famous people. Use these adjectives or suggest some of your own.

beautiful	fast	friendly
good-looking	interesting	talented

Compare: Matt Dillon / Johnny Depp
Hilary Duff / Nicole Richie
Beyoncé / Shakira
Andy Roddick / Rafael Nadal

Useful language:
- In my opinion, . . .
- Some people think that . . . but I . . .
- Do you think so?
- I can't argue with that.
- I agree / don't agree with you. I think . . . is far more talented.

GRAMMAR FOCUS

Double comparatives:
the . . . the . . .

Cause	Effect
The **bigger** the waves,	the **better** the surfing.

Meaning: When the waves are bigger, the surfing is better.

The **more** you study, the **more** you learn.
The **longer** she waits, the **angrier** she gets.

Discovering grammar

Look at the grammar chart. Write the meanings of the examples.

1. *When the waves are bigger, the surfing is better.*
2. *When you*
3. *When she*

Practicing grammar

9 Practice

Rewrite the sentences. Use double comparatives.

1. When the waves are bigger, the surfing is better.
   The bigger the waves, the better the surfing.
2. When she gets very tired, she becomes more stressed.
   The more tired she gets, the more stressed she becomes.
3. When she drives faster, I get more and more nervous.
4. When the coffee is fresh, the taste is better.
5. When I exercise more often, I get stronger.

10 Communication

Make comparisons

A. **A48** Listen and read.

   A: Last year's championship game was much more exciting than this year's.
   B: Do you think so? Why?
   A: Last year's players were a lot better.
   B: Well, I can't argue with that. The better the players, the more exciting the game.

B. **PAIRS.** Role-play the conversation.

11 Your turn

A. **PAIRS.** Choose a sport. In your notebook, write sentences about it using double comparatives.

   For example:

   The better the _____, the better the _____.

   The more you _____, the better you _____.

   The easier the _____, the more you _____.

   The farther the _____, the more you _____.

B. **CLASS.** Share your sentences with the class.

12 Writing

A. Write a paragraph about the sport you chose for Exercise 11. Include the following:

   - Name of the sport
   - Where it's played
   - Favorite player or players
   - How to score points
   - How to win (use double comparatives)

B. **PAIRS.** Read and comment on your classmate's writing. Use the Peer editing checklist on page 134 to help you.

13 Reading

A49 Listen and read the results of a study on the differences between men and women drivers. As you read, think about this question: Who do you think are worse drivers, men or women?

Who takes the greatest risks?
by Gary Parkinson

Men are far worse drivers than women, says a report from an automobile association. Men take risks. They are more likely to drink alcohol before driving, and they have accidents much more frequently than women.

According to the report, women like the independence of driving, while men like the thrill they get behind the steering wheel of a car. In general, men are less concerned about danger. They drive faster and overtake other vehicles more frequently than women of the same age and driving experience.

Although speed is one of the most common causes of accidents, men think that breaking the speed limit is a minor offense. Furthermore, men are more prepared to drive long distances without a break, and they are more impatient than women. If men want the car in front of them to speed up or to get out of the way, they follow it closely, often flashing their headlights and honking.

The study also shows that age seems to be a factor. There is new evidence that young men drive less safely than any other group. "The young believe they react faster, but the truth is that they are slower than older people to detect dangers," says Professor McKenna, the author of the study. "In fact, the older you get, the more careful you become."

14 Comprehension

Answer the questions.

1. What is the report's conclusion about men and women drivers?
2. Give at least three reasons why men are considered worse drivers than women.

15 Speaking

GROUPS. Discuss the following questions.

1. Do you agree with the study when it says that men are worse drivers than women? Why or why not?
2. Do you believe that "the older you get, the more careful you become"?

16 Vocabulary
Word building

A. Some words can be transformed from one part of speech to another by adding or taking away *suffixes* (letters added to the end of a word to form a new word). Study the words in the chart. Then fill in the rest of the chart. You may use a dictionary.

Noun	Adjective	Adverb
1. independence	independent	independently
2. danger	dangerous	dangerously
3. care	careful	carefully
4. care	careless	carelessly
5. impatience	impatient	
6. courage		
7. weakness		
8. jealousy		

B. **A50** Listen and repeat the words in the chart. Check your answers.

C. Fill in the blanks. Use words from Exercise A.

1. A: I'm proud of Sam for being so ___courageous___.
   B: Yes, he acted ___courageously___, didn't he?

2. A: You're good at skateboarding. But I think you ride your skateboard _____.
   B: Maybe. But to me, the more _____ the trick, the more fun it is.

3. A: Please be _____ when you drive today. The roads are wet.
   B: You know me. I always drive _____.

4. A: Come on! Hurry up!
   B: You're so _____!
   A: I'm sorry. My mom always says that _____ is one of my worse faults.

17 Listening

A. **A51** Listen to the conversation. Put a check (✓) next to the comparative adjectives you hear.

- ☐ more independent
- ☑ more popular
- ☐ more impatient
- ☐ more daring
- ☐ more creative
- ☐ more careless
- ☐ more courageous
- ☐ more adventurous

B. **A52** Try to complete the sentences using the adjectives you heard. Then listen again and check your answers.

1. The show is ___much more popular___ now than it was a few years ago.
2. Boys are _____ and take far more risks.
3. Boys are not _____ than girls.
4. Boys are usually _____ than girls.

Learn to learn

Build vocabulary using visualization.

Try to use new words in a sentence that you can visualize. This will help you remember the word and its meaning.

Select a new word from this unit that you want to learn. In your personal dictionary or on a separate piece of paper, write your sentence and draw a picture of it.

nervous / nervously

Nervous Nell looked nervously at the mouse.

48 Unit 5

Putting it together *Walk of Fame*

A. 🅐53 Read along as you listen. What's Scott's opinion of California?

1. Look! There's Marilyn Monroe's star . . . I'm glad we came, aren't you, Jack?

Yeah, but I'm not so sure about those two. Scott looks bored and Kelly looks a lot more upset now.

2. I've been thinking about Scott. I'm not sure I like him.

Well, I *know* I don't like him. He thinks he's the king of the surfing world.

3. I really think Hawaii is better than California. The waves are much more powerful there. And we have far better surfers there, too.

You really can't stop bragging, can you?

4. Did you hear that? What did I tell you?

Shh, Jack. Lower your voice.

5. Are you still mad at me because I canceled our date? Kelly, I've apologized a million times!

Can we talk about something else?

Like what? Marilyn Monroe?

6. Hey, guys. Cool place, isn't it? Are you enjoying yourselves back there?

B. GROUPS. Discuss these questions: Why is Kelly unhappy with Scott? How do Denise and Jack feel about Scott?

Unit 5   49

Game 2 Tag relay

You need:
- a coin
- a game piece (such as an eraser)

Steps:

1. Divide the class into teams of two players each.

2. All the teams start playing when the teacher says *Go*. One team member flips a coin. (Heads is two moves, tails is one move.) That person moves his or her game piece and asks a tag question based on the box he or she lands on. An *X* is a negative statement with an affirmative tag (*You're not a surfer, are you?*) and an *O* is an affirmative statement with a negative tag (*You can swim, can't you?*).

3. The other team member answers the question using his or her own information (*Yes, I am. / No, I'm not. etc.*), flips the coin, moves his or her game piece, and asks a question. Students continue taking turns and moving forward along the board.

4. The first team to land on "Finish" stands and asks, *We've won, haven't we?*

Useful language
- I'm not sure how to answer this.
- No, that's not right.
- Great job!

START	X Been to Florida	O A good dancer	X Going to snow tomorrow	O Have a new girl/boyfriend
X A surfer	Go forward 2 spaces	X Like to sing in the shower	O Going to buy me a present	X Like spiders
O Can swim	X Sleepy	FINISH	X Have a dog	Go back 1 space
X Took the bus this morning	O Like sushi	X Went shopping last week	Go back 2 spaces	O Want to be an actor
O Always do your homework	Go forward 1 space	X Play the piano	O Watched TV last night	X Raining outside now

50 Game 2

Project 2 — A snapshot of pros and cons

PAIRS. Work together to compare two places or things. Use the steps below as a guide. Present your report to the class.

1. Choose two things you want to compare, such as:
   - country life and city life
   - vacation spots
   - products
   - movies

2. Brainstorm differences and similarities, pros (advantages) and cons (disadvantages). Take notes.

   City life for teens: more to do, getting around is easier

   Country life for teens: more relaxing, more privacy

   Both: have benefits for teens

3. Design a chart that you can present to your group or class.

   Comparing life for teens in the city and the country

	City	Country	Both
noisy	✔		
cheap		✔	
activities	✔		
transportation	✔		
privacy		✔	
benefits for teens			✔

4. Present your report in front of your group or class. Use your chart as a point of reference. Take turns speaking about your chart.

   Our report compares life for teenagers in the city and the country. Both the city and the country are nice places to live, and they each have benefits for teens.

   Living in the city can be more exciting than living in the country. There is always something to do or somewhere to go. For example, on a Saturday afternoon you can go to the movies, go to museums, or go shopping. And getting around in the city is easy. You can take public transportation like buses or the subway—you don't need a car. But there are also some disadvantages to living in the city. The city is usually dirtier than the country. There are more cars and people, so there is more pollution. The city is also noisier than the country.

   There may not be as many activities for teens in the country, but there are still some activities that teens can enjoy. In the country you can go bike riding, horseback riding, and hiking. Also, houses in the country are usually bigger than in the city.

6 Will you be needing it later?

1 Reading

A54 Read along as you listen to the timeline below. What do you think computers will be doing for people in the future?

2 Comprehension

Answer the questions.

1. List the key inventions in information technology between 1970 and the mid 1990s.
2. How did the Internet change the way people live?
3. How might homes and computers change in the future?

Learning goals

Communication
Talk about future possibilities in technology

Grammar
The future: *will* + verb and *be going to* + verb
The future continuous: *will be* + verb *-ing*

Vocabulary
Computer terms

INFORMATION TECHNOLOGY TIMELINE

1970s through the 1980s
In 1972, the first e-mail program successfully transmitted a message. Later, IBM introduced its personal computer (PC) for use in the home, office, and schools. Video games hit the market.

Early-Mid 1990s
The World Wide Web (www) became a reality. In 1996, David Filo and Jerry Yang officially launched their site, Yahoo!, the first navigational guide to the Web.

Late 1990s–2000s
The Internet connects people in 150 countries around the world. People are able to work from home (telecommute), using the phone and the Internet. Students use the Internet in school. A "global village" exists on the Internet.

Present–2020s
Over the next twenty years or so, people will be moving into fully computerized homes. Television, telephones, and computers will become totally integrated.

2030 and beyond
Computers will become conscious, like human beings. They will be doing more and more things that previously only human beings could do. For example, they will be learning from their own experiences.

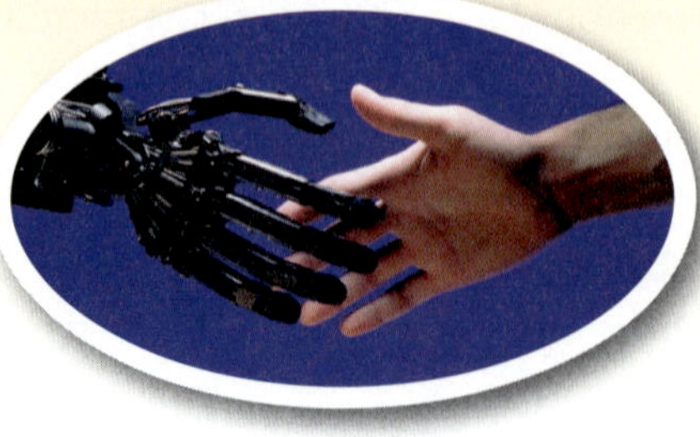

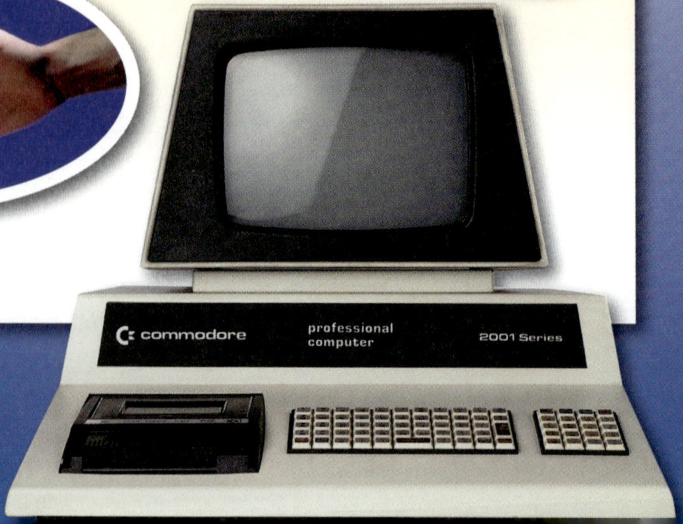

52 Unit 6

GRAMMAR FOCUS

The future: *will* + verb and *be going to* + verb

	Affirmative statements	Negative statements
Prediction:	Hopefully **we'll have** fun at the party.	It **won't be** boring.
	I think it**'s going to be** fun.	It**'s not going to be** boring.
Intention/Plan:	I**'m going to invite** Jack to the party.	I**'m not going to invite** Manolo.
Promise:	I**'ll be** here if you need me.	I **won't leave** you.
Decision:	I**'ll have** pizza and a soda.	I **won't have** dessert.

Discovering grammar

Look at the grammar chart. Use *will* + verb or *be going to* + verb to complete the grammar rules.

1. When you predict the future, use _____ or _____.
2. When you describe a plan that you have already made, use _____.
3. When you announce a decision made at the moment of speaking, use _____.
4. When you make a promise about the future, use _____.

Practicing grammar

3 Practice

A. Circle the correct answers.

Waiter: Can I take your order?
Darren: (**1.** *I'll* / *I'm going to*) have lasagna with french fries and a salad.
Dulcie: That sounds like far too much, Darren! (**2.** *You won't* / *You aren't going to*) eat all that!
Darren: Who says? Anyway, (**3.** *I'll* / *I'm going to*) have dessert, too. Ice cream.
Waiter: And for you, Miss?
Dulcie: Sorry, I haven't decided yet.
Waiter: That's OK. (**4.** *I'll* / *I'm going to*) come back in a couple of minutes.
Dulcie: So, are you planning to sit there playing that computer game all evening?
Darren: Mmm?
Dulcie: I can see this (**5.** *will* / *is going to*) be a fun night out.

B. 🔊 A55 Listen and check your answers.

4 Practice

Fill in the blanks with *will* or *be going to* and the verbs in parentheses.

1. **A:** Excuse me. Can you help me, please?
   B: I (*be*) *'ll be* right with you.
2. **A:** What are your plans for this summer?
   B: I (*visit*) _____ my grandparents.
3. **A:** I need to be at the airport by 7:00 P.M.
   B: OK. We (*leave*) _____ the house at 5:00 P.M.
4. **A:** What would you like to order?
   B: I (*have*) _____ the lunch special.
5. **A:** Who do you think (*win*) _____?
   B: I think the Italian team (*win*) _____.

Unit 6 53

5 Dialogue

A56 Cover the dialogue and listen.

Kelly: Excuse me, Aunt Paula. How long will you be using the computer?
Aunt Paula: I'm about to log off . . . Here you go. It's all yours.
Kelly: Thanks. I need to search the Internet, so I'll be using the computer for a while. Will you be needing it later?
Aunt Paula: Not until tonight.
Kelly: Great! I just need to get some information.
Aunt Paula: OK.
Kelly: Uh . . . , can I take next Saturday off?
Aunt Paula: Kelly, you know weekends are our busiest time. Why?
Kelly: We're going to go to Universal Studios.
Aunt Paula: "We" meaning . . . ?
Kelly: Denise, Jack, and, er . . . Scott.
Aunt Paula: I see. Well, not on a Saturday. Why don't you go on Monday?
Kelly: That might work. I'll check with the group. Thanks!

6 Comprehension

A. Answer the questions.

1. What are the two reasons that Kelly wants to talk to Aunt Paula?
2. Where does Kelly plan to go?
3. Why can't Kelly take Saturday off?

B. **A57** Read along as you listen again. Check your answers.

7 Useful expressions

A. **A58** Listen and repeat.
- It's all yours.
- for a while
- "We" meaning . . . ?
- That might work.

B. Reorder the lines to make a conversation.

____ Well, I'm doing a project, too, so I can't stop. Use Dad's laptop.
____ Not yet. Why?
____ That might work. I'll ask him.
____ "We" meaning . . . ?
_1_ Are you about to log off?
____ Gustavo and I. We have to work on our school project.
____ Because we need to use the computer for a while.

C. **PAIRS.** Memorize the conversation. Then role-play it from memory.

54 Unit 6

8 Vocabulary

Computer terms

Complete the definitions with words and phrases from the box. Then complete the crossword puzzle.

| close | delete | ~~download~~ | drag | log off |
| log on | open | save | search | surf |

ACROSS

1. To _download_ is to move information onto your computer system.
4. To _____ a file is to end using a certain file.
6. To _____ is to stop using a specific computer program.
7. To _____ the Internet is to look for specific information on the Internet.
8. To _____ a file is to find a certain file and begin using it.

DOWN

1. To _____ is to remove a piece of information from a computer's memory.
2. To _____ an item is to physically move it from one place to another.
3. To _____ the Internet is to look quickly at different websites on the Internet.
5. To _____ is to start using a computer by typing a certain word (a password).
7. To _____ is to make a computer keep the work that you have done on it.

9 Pronunciation

Stress in phrasal verbs

A. **A59** Listen. Underline the word in the phrasal verb with the strongest stress.

1. take off
2. try out
3. turn on
4. turn off
5. log on
6. log off
7. keep up
8. be into

B. **A60** Read the sentences and underline the phrasal verbs. Then listen and repeat each sentence.

1. Do you like to try out new electronic gadgets?
2. My brother and I are into computer games.
3. Will you turn off your cell phone, please?
4. My sister can't log on. She forgot her password.
5. It's not easy to keep up with technology.

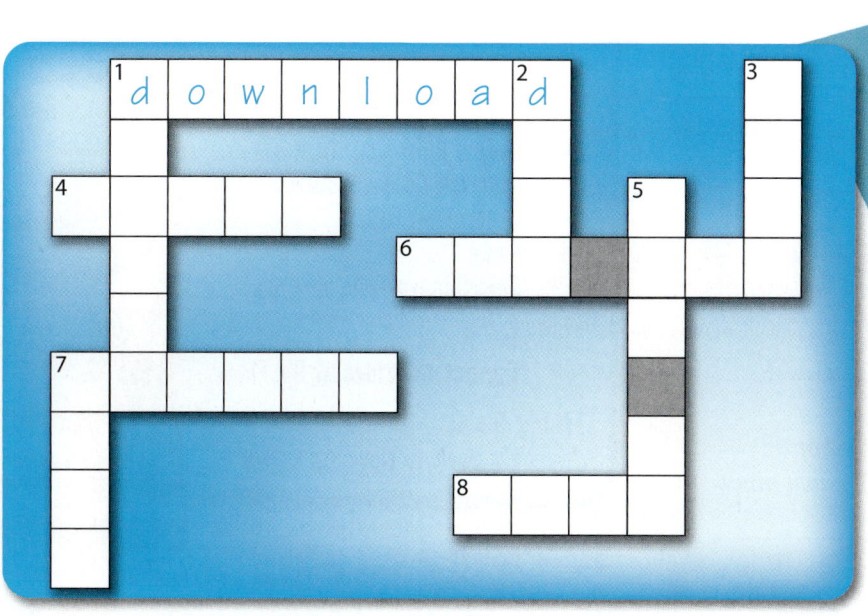

Unit 6 55

GRAMMAR FOCUS

The future continuous: *will be* + verb *-ing*

Affirmative statement
Kelly **will be searching** the Internet all afternoon.

Negative statement
She **will not (won't) be working**.

Yes / No question
Will you **be needing** the computer later?

Short answer
Yes, I **will**. / No, I **won't**.

Information question
What **will** we **be doing** from 1–3 P.M.?

Discovering grammar

Look at the grammar chart. Circle the correct answers.

1. Use the future continuous to describe (*a quick action* / *an action taking place over a period of time*) in the future.
2. To form the future continuous, use *will be* + (*the base form* / *the -ing form*) of the verb.

Practicing grammar

10 Practice

Complete the conversations below. Use the future continuous and the cues.

1. **A:** My family's going to Great Adventure tomorrow!
   B: I'm so jealous. While you're having fun, (*I / clean / the house*) <u>I'll be cleaning the house</u>.

2. **A:** I can't wait till summer vacation.
   B: Just think. Two months from now (*we / relax / on the beach*) _____.

3. **A:** I'm going over to the clothes department.
   B: OK. While you're doing that, (*I / hang out / in the music department*) _____.

4. **A:** Can I check my e-mail before we go?
   B: OK. But (*we / wait / in the car*) _____, so hurry up.

5. **A:** I think David's going to be a star.
   B: Me, too. In a few years (*we / watch him / on TV*) _____.

11 Practice

PAIRS. Imagine you are going on a trip. Use the schedule to ask and answer questions.

A: What will we be doing on Thursday?
B: We'll be trying out the rides at Six Flags.

Holiday Adventure

Tuesday, 8–11 A.M.
Travel by bus from New York City to Cooperstown
1–4 P.M.
Visit the Baseball Hall of Fame

Wednesday, 8:30 A.M.–12 P.M.
Go from Cooperstown to Niagara Falls
1–4 P.M.
See Niagara Falls up close

Thursday, 9 A.M.–4 P.M.
Try out the rides at Six Flags

Friday, 9 A.M.
Fly back to New York City

12 Practice

Have a competition! Go to page 131.

TEEN TALK

PAIRS. Talk with a classmate about what you plan to do this weekend.

Useful language:
- I'm going to . . .
- How about you? What will you be doing Saturday afternoon?
- Are you going to . . . ?
- I don't really have any plans yet.
- I'll be doing my homework on Sunday.
- Me, too.

Learn to learn

Review your writing goals.

Always know what your goals are when you are assigned a writing task. After writing a first draft, check to see how well you expressed yourself and how well you achieved your writing goals.

Refer to this checklist for the writing task in Exercise 14:

- Did I include the important information in the announcement?
- Does my announcement have a strong opening and closing?
- Did I use persuasive language?

13 Your turn

A. Write your own resolutions and predictions.

My resolution for next year:
1. I'm going to study harder.
2. _____
3. _____
4. _____

My predictions for the world:
1. The world's population will rise.
2. _____
3. _____
4. _____

My predictions about what will be happening by a certain date:
1. By 2050, the world will be using much more solar energy.
2. _____
3. _____
4. _____

B. GROUPS. Read each other's resolutions and predictions. Ask and answer questions about them.

14 Writing

GROUPS. Imagine you own an electronics store, and you are about to have your "grand opening." Write a radio announcement to tell people about the opening of your new store. Follow these steps:

1. Discuss what kind of electronics your store will specialize in (cell phones, computers, gadgets, etc.).
2. Decide what you want to say in your radio announcement. Be sure to include the name of the store, when it's opening, the kinds of items you will be selling, and a reason for people to come to your store. Give your announcement a strong opening and closing, and use persuasive language.

For example:
- We'll have the lowest prices in town!
- You won't have to shop anywhere else. Not anywhere else!
- You'll find the latest products, the highest quality, and the lowest prices!
- Why don't you come and see us today?

3. Write a draft of your announcement. Then review it. Make sure you've included all the points mentioned above. Revise your draft, as needed.
4. Present your radio announcement to the class.

15 Communication

Talk about future possibilities in technology

A. 🔊 **A61** Listen and read.

A: Have you ever heard of "smart houses"?
B: No. What are they?
A: They're houses that do your chores for you. People will be living in them 20 years from now.
B: So, in 20 years people won't be doing chores anymore?
A: No, they won't. Their houses will be planning and preparing meals, and they'll even be cleaning themselves!
B: That's awesome!

B. PAIRS. Write a conversation about a future possibility in technology. Use *will* + verb, *be going to* + verb, and the future continuous. Role-play the conversation.

For example:

A: Have you ever heard of "smart refrigerators"?
B: No, I haven't. What are they?
A: . . .

16 Listening

🔊 **A62** Jake, an executive at a music company (or "label") is speaking at a school about music and the future. Listen and fill in the blanks.

1. Napster was a popular website where people could _____.
2. _____ and _____ weren't happy about the website, so they sued the company.
3. Now people pay a fee for each _____ download.
4. Generally, people can pay a fee for each song or pay a _____ fee for an unlimited number of songs.
5. The speaker thinks that in the future people will be buying _____ albums from stores.

17 Speaking

GROUPS. Some people think songs and movies should be available on the Web for free. Some people think it is important to charge for each song or movie that is downloaded. How do you feel about this subject? Discuss these questions.

1. If you were a songwriter, would you want people to download your music without paying you?
2. Should older songs be free, while newer songs cost money to download?
3. Should all movies be free to download from the Internet?

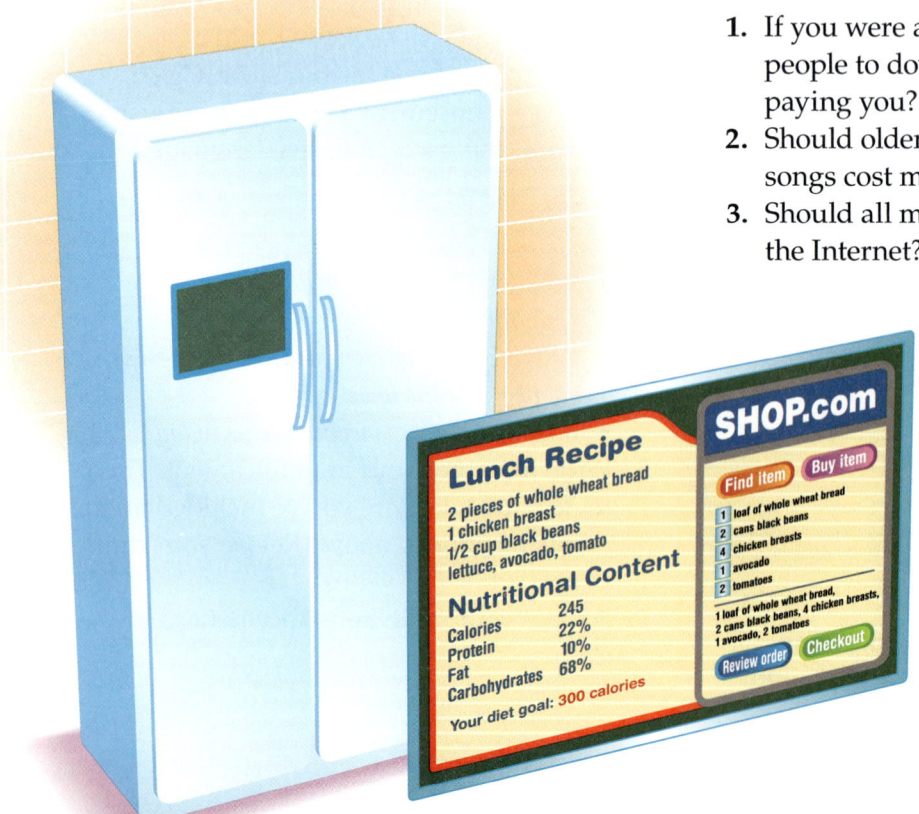

Progress check Units 5 and 6

> **Test-taking tip:** Don't get stuck on one item. If you don't know an answer, skip it and come back to it later. Later, if you're still unsure, decide what the *best* answer is. Try to guess wisely.

Grammar

A. Circle the correct answer to complete each statement. (3 points each)

1. **A:** Do you like surfing the Internet?
   B: Yes, I do. It's (*much more* / *a lot*) fun than watching TV.
2. **A:** Do you study a lot?
   B: Yes. The more I study, the (*more* / *most*) I learn.
3. **A:** Why did you leave so soon?
   B: I finished the test more (*quick* / *quickly*) than the other students.
4. **A:** Why do you go to the gym so often?
   B: I go because the more I exercise, (*I feel better* / *the better I feel*).

B. Complete each sentence with the correct comparative or superlative adverb. Use the adverbs in parentheses. (4 points each)

I was late for school, so I got out of bed (1. *quick*) _more quickly_ than I usually do. I wasn't feeling very well, and I had slept (2. *late*) _____ than I should have. But after breakfast I felt even (3. *bad*) _____, so I decided not to go to school. I went back to bed. When I woke up at ten o'clock, I was feeling a little (4. *good*) _____. I slept ten more hours that day. That's (5. *long*) _____ I've ever slept in my life!

C. Read the statements. Then complete the sentences using the future continuous tense and the cues. (3 points each)

1. Don't call me at seven. (*I / have*)
   I'll be having dinner then.
2. My sister has her driver's test tomorrow. She really wants to pass the test.
   (*She / drive*) _____ very carefully tomorrow.
3. A big storm is coming. (*Schools / close*)
   _____ early today.
4. Pedro has to clean his apartment before the party tomorrow. (*He / clean*)
   _____ all afternoon.
5. Alice plans to do a lot of dancing at Pedro's party tomorrow. (*She / dance*)
   _____ all night.

Vocabulary

D. Write *True* or *False*. (2 points each)

True 1. When you search the Internet, you want specific information.
_____ 2. You always save files you will never look at again.
_____ 3. You can download files from the Internet.
_____ 4. When you delete a file, you will be able to use it later.
_____ 5. When you're finished using a computer, you log on.

Communication

E. Complete the conversation with responses using the future continuous. Use your imagination. (5 points)

A: What do you think you'll be doing ten years from now?
B: I think I'll be . . .
A: Will you be living in the same town?
B: No, I won't. I'll . . .

Now I can . . .
❏ give emphasis to my comparisons.
❏ talk about future possibilities.
❏ talk about how to use a computer.

Unit 6   59

Wide Angle on the world

1 Reading

> **Reading skill:** Finding topic sentences
> An important skill for reading is finding the main idea. The main idea is often expressed in a topic sentence.

A. **PAIRS.** Skim the article. Find the sentence that tells what the article will be about and underline it. Compare your answer with your classmate's answer.

B. Write *True* or *False* for each statement. Then read the article and check your answers.

　　＿＿＿＿ 1. In the future, it may be possible for computers to understand how we feel.

　　＿＿＿＿ 2. Computers help scientists study people's emotional health.

　　＿＿＿＿ 3. When people are face-to-face, most of the communication happens through speaking.

　　＿＿＿＿ 4. Scientists have invented an MP3 player that can tell when you're sad.

2 Speaking

GROUPS. Is a computer that identifies human emotions a good idea or a bad idea? Discuss and give examples that support your point of view. Take notes on the discussion. Then share your opinions with the class.

3 Writing

Use your notes from the discussion in Exercise 2 to write a paragraph about the advantages and disadvantages of a computer that can identify human emotions.

4 Listening

A63 Listen to the radio commercial. Then answer the questions.
1. How often does the wireless newspaper "The Wave" update stories?
2. In what cities can you get local news on "The Wave"?
3. How many sheets of plastic make up "The Wave"?
4. How much does the first six months cost if you sign up this week?

EMOTIONAL ELECTRONICS

Computers are important communication tools. The Internet helps people interact with one another when they can't be face-to-face. E-mails, blogs, and instant messages (IMs) are popular ways to communicate using the Internet. But even though computers help us, they are only machines that can't really understand us ... or can they? Have you ever shouted in anger at a computer? What if the computer could hear you and respond to your anger? Scientists predict that in the near future, computers may be able to do just that.

Scientists are already developing computers that can recognize human emotions. Take LifeShirt, for example. LifeShirt is a computerized shirt that is worn day and night. It collects data that helps scientists study a person's health condition, including their emotional health.

In the future, it may be possible for computers not only to recognize people's emotions, but also to predict their behavior. When people are face-to-face, most communication happens without speaking, through body language. Computers will interpret body language and use that data. For example, in a social situation, they may be able to predict whether or not someone will go on a date with you!

But that's not all. Scientists predict that one day, computers will automatically respond to our human emotions. If you're hungry, your computer will suggest it's time for a snack. If you feel sad, your MP3 player might cheer you up with your favorite song.

Recognize our emotions ... *predict* our emotions ... *respond to* our emotions ... what's next? One day, will computers be able to *influence* our emotions?

7 If I were you, I'd...

1 Dialogue

B2 Cover the dialogue and listen.

Matt: Jack, can you take me to the movies tomorrow?
Jack: No way! I'm going out with Denise next Monday.
Matt: So what? That's a week away.
Jack: I know, wise guy. But we're going to Universal Studios, so I have to save money.
Matt: Universal Studios? With Denise?
Jack: Yeah. Scott and Kelly are going, too.
Matt: I wish I could go with you. That'd be awesome!
Jack: If I had enough money, I'd take you. Maybe Mom will give you some if you ask her nicely.
Matt: Will you come with me and ask?
Jack: OK, but if I go with you, will you promise to stop messing around with my computer?
Matt: I promise. Do you think Mom will give me the money?
Jack: You never know. If I were you, I'd go right now. Come on!

Learning goals

Communication
Talk about imaginary situations

Grammar
First conditional
Second conditional
I wish + the simple past: Expressing wishes for a present situation

Vocabulary
Phrasal verbs with *go*

2 Comprehension

A. Answer the questions.

1. What news does Jack tell Matt?
2. What's Matt's reaction to the news?
3. What does Jack agree to do with Matt?
4. What does Matt promise to do?

B. **B3** Read along as you listen again. Check your answers.

3 Useful expressions

A. **B4** Listen and repeat.
- No way!
- So what?
- wise guy
- That'd be awesome.
- You never know.

B. Complete the conversation with expressions from Exercise A.

A: Are you going out with Nela tonight?
B: Yeah. We're seeing Brad and Angela for dinner.
A: OK, ____wise guy____. What are you really doing?
B: We're going to see the new IMAX movie. Do you want to come with us?
A: _____ But I don't have a date.
B: _____ That doesn't matter. Come alone.
A: No, thanks.
B: Well, maybe Tanya will go with you.
A: _____ She'd never say yes to me.
B: Ask her. _____ She might say yes.

C. **PAIRS.** Role-play the conversation.

4 Vocabulary

Phrasal verbs with *go*

A. **B5** Listen and repeat. Then use your dictionary to match the phrasal verbs with their meanings.

__c__ 1. go out   a. break a promise
____ 2. go out with   b. try to do or get something
____ 3. go over   c. leave your house
____ 4. go against   d. continue
____ 5. go back on   e. have a date with someone
____ 6. go for   f. review, look at carefully
____ 7. go on   g. agree with
____ 8. go along with h. do the opposite of

B. **PAIRS.** Complete the sentences.

1. Did Denise go __along with__ the plan?
2. Jack is going _____ Denise.
3. I'm going _____ to get some ice cream. Do you want to come?
4. He likes to make promises, but he always goes _____ them.
5. Always go _____ your answers.
6. Go _____. Don't stop talking.
7. His mom is very strict. He never goes _____ her wishes.
8. Don't be afraid to try. Go _____ your goals.

Learn to learn

Find definitions in a dictionary.

Many words have more than one definition in the dictionary. The definitions are numbered. The most common use of the word is listed first.

Look at the definitions for the phrasal verb *go for*. Which definition matches the one in Exercise 4?

go for
1: to want or like something
2: to choose a particular thing
3: to try to get or win something

Unit 7 63

GRAMMAR FOCUS

First conditional: *If* clauses in future-time situations

| If the weather is nice on Saturday, they If it's not raining on Saturday, they | will, are going to, may, might, can, could | go to Universal Studios. |

Discovering grammar

Look at the grammer chart. Read each sentence and write *True* or *False*.

_____ 1. You can use the simple present or the present continuous in an *if* clause to show future meaning.

_____ 2. You can use *will* + verb or *be going to* + verb in an *if* clause to show future meaning.

Practicing grammar

5 Practice

Use the cues to answer the questions below.

1. *will / won't*
   What will you do if there's no school tomorrow? (go to Grandma's)
   If there's no school tomorrow, I'll go to Grandma's.

2. *can*
   What will we do if the bookstore is closed? (go to the library)
   _____
   _____

3. *may / might*
   What will happen if the game is cancelled? (have to play on Friday instead)
   _____
   _____

4. *be going to*
   What is she going to do if she fails the test? (take it again next year)
   _____
   _____

6 Practice

In your notebook, write sentences using the pros and cons below.

Should I go traveling with my friends this summer?	
Pros (advantages)	**Cons (disadvantages)**
see interesting places	spend too much money
meet people from different cultures	miss my friends at home
learn new things	have no time to relax

For example:

Pros
- *If I go traveling, I'll see some interesting places.*

Cons
- *If I go traveling, I might spend too much money.*

7 Listening

B6 Listen to the conversation. Then complete the sentences.

1. If Jenny gets up early enough, she *might go skateboarding*.
2. If David goes to Jack's house, he _____.
3. If the movie is scary, Jenny _____.
4. If the baseball game is on, David _____.

64 Unit 7

Grammar Focus

Second conditional:
If clauses in imaginary situations

If I **were** you, I**'d go** right now.	I**'d go** right now **if** I **were** you.
If I **had** some money, I **could go**, too.	I **could go** too **if** I **had** some money.
If I **went** to Universal Studios, I **might see** someone famous.	I **might see** someone famous **if** I **went** to Universal Studios.

Discovering grammar

Look at the grammar chart. Circle the correct answers.

1. For imaginary situations, which tense appears in the *if* clause?
   a. the simple present   b. the simple past
2. For imaginary situations, which clause has *would*, *could*, or *might* + base form of the verb?
   a. the *if* clause   b. the result clause
3. Look at these two sentences. Which is more likely to happen, a or b?
   a. *If I have time, I'll come over to your house.*
   b. *If I had time, I'd come over to your house.*

Practicing grammar

8 Practice

Rewrite the sentences using *if* clauses in imaginary situations.

1. If there's enough space in our new apartment, Dad might buy an aquarium. (There isn't enough space in our new apartment.)
   If there were enough space in our new apartment,
   Dad might buy an aquarium.

2. If I have the day off Saturday, I'll go to the beach. (But I don't have the day off.)
   _____

3. If you speak French, you can enjoy French TV shows. (But you don't speak French.)
   _____

4. Martina will lend you $100 if she has money. (She doesn't have money.)
   _____

5. If the weather is nice, we can go biking. (The weather isn't nice.)
   _____

9 Practice

Have a competition! Go to page 132.

10 Pronunciation

Intonation in sentences with *if* clauses

A. **B7** Listen. Pay attention to the intonation pattern at the end of each clause.

If my cousins lived closer,
I'd see them more often.

B. **B8** Listen and repeat. Match the intonation pattern.

1. If I played in that band, I'd definitely be the star.
2. If he had enough money, he'd buy a new car.
3. If she weren't so busy, she'd go out with you.
4. If the puppy behaved, it could ride in the car.
5. If I were you, I'd wait until tomorrow.

Unit 7   65

11 Your turn

A. GROUPS. Take turns asking the questions in the box below. Choose a group member to record your group's responses.

1. What would you do if you were the principal of your school?
2. What would you be if you could have any job in the world?
3. What would you do if you were the leader of your country?
4. Where would you live if you could live anywhere in the world?
5. What would you do if you had a lot of money?

B. CLASS. Share your group's responses with the class.

12 Writing

A. Choose a question from Exercise 11. In your notebook, explain what you would do if you were in that situation.

> If I could live anywhere in the world, I'd live on one of the islands in Hawaii. I'd probably choose to live on the island of Oahu. If I lived on Oahu, I'd sit on the beach every day and watch surfers surf...

B. CLASS. Read your paragraph to the class.

13 Communication

Talk about imaginary situations

A. 🎧 **B9** Listen and read.

A: What would your life be like if you didn't have to go to school?
B: It'd be really cool. I could sleep until ten o'clock. Then I'd watch TV all afternoon.
A: Wouldn't you get bored?
B: No way. I love TV.

B. PAIRS. Write a conversation about a situation that is unlikely to happen. Role-play the conversation.

Unit 7

GRAMMAR FOCUS

**I wish + the simple past:
Expressing wishes for a present situation**

I wish I **were** taller (but I'm not).
I wish you **lived** closer to me (but you don't).
I wish we **played** on that team (but we don't).
I wish she **played** on our team (but she doesn't).
I wish we **didn't live** near the airport (but we do).
I wish I **could speak** Italian (but I can't).

Discovering grammar

Look at the grammar chart. Circle the correct answer.

Use *I wish* + the simple past to make wishes about _____.
(*the past / the present*)

Practicing grammar

14 Practice

Complete the sentence with the past tense form of a verb from the box.

| be | can play | ~~know~~ | not feel | live | have |

1. I wish I ___knew___ more jokes.
2. I wish Leo _____ in my class.
3. I wish I _____ a bigger backpack for all my new school books.
4. I wish we _____ in San Diego where it's warm all year.
5. I wish I _____ an instrument.
6. I wish I _____ so tired.

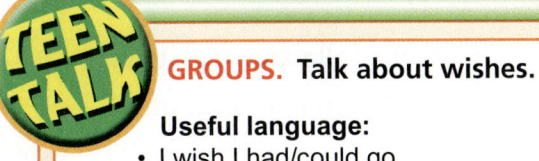

TEEN TALK

GROUPS. Talk about wishes.

Useful language:
- I wish I had/could go . . .
- I think a lot of kids wish they could . . .
- Most people wish there were . . .
- I think so, too.
- I'm not sure I agree with you.

15 Practice

Read the situations. Then write sentences. Use cues from the box.

| be taller | not have to babysit |
| have some money | |

1. You're thirsty. You don't have any money with you.

   I wish I had money.
   Then I could buy something to drink.

2. You want to ride the Tornado 2000. You aren't tall enough.

   _____.
   Then I could ride the Tornado 2000.

3. Your friends are having a party tonight. You have to babysit your little sister.

   _____.
   Then I could go to the party.

Unit 7 67

16 Reading

B10 Read along silently as you listen. Underline Severn's challenge to adults.

Changing the World

If you were 12 years old, would you try to change the world? And if you had only six minutes to change the world, would you still try? Severn Cullis-Suzuki from Canada did. She was 12 years old when she spoke for six minutes at the Earth Summit in Rio de Janeiro in 1992.

Below is part of that speech:

"I am only a child. Yet I know that if all the money spent on war were spent on ending poverty and finding environmental answers, what a wonderful place this would be. In school, you teach us not to fight with others, to work things out, to respect others, to clean up our mess, not to hurt other creatures, to share, not to be greedy. Then why do you go out and do the things you tell us not to do? You grown-ups say you love us, but I challenge you, please, to make your actions reflect your words . . .

. . . In Canada, we lead the good life with plenty of food, water, and shelter. We have watches, bicycles, television sets, and computers—the list could go on for pages.

[Recently, we met] some children living on the street. This is what one of them told us: 'I wish I were rich; and if I were, I would give all the street children food, clothes, medicine, shelter, and love and affection.'

If a child on the street who has nothing is willing to share, why are we who have everything still so greedy?"

Severn received a standing ovation, and people in the audience cried. Today, Severn continues to fight for the environment. She is a member of a United Nations World Summit advisory panel and travels around the world giving speeches.

17 Comprehension

Answer the questions.

1. Why was Severn in Rio de Janeiro in 1992?
2. Why did she criticize adults?
3. How was her life in Canada different from the lives of the street children that she met?
4. What was the audience's reaction to her speech?

18 Speaking

GROUPS. Discuss the following question.

Do you agree with Severn that adults don't "practice what they preach," or do what they tell others to do? Give examples to support your answer.

Putting it together — Negotiating with Mom

A. B11 Listen and read. How much money is Matt going to earn?

1.
- Hi, Mom. Matt wants to ask you something.
- OK. What is it?

2.
- Can I go to Universal Studios with Jack and Denise?
- If it's OK with Jack, sure. Do you have any money?
- A little. Around ten dollars.

3.
- If I had more money, Mom, I'd pay for him, but I don't.
- I see. Well, Matt, maybe you could work for Dad and me?

4.
- And will you pay me?
- Of course. If you did some work around the house. . . .

5.
- Like what kind of work, Mom?
- Well, if you washed Dad's car, and if you helped me do the laundry . . .
- How much could I earn?

6.
- Is ten dollars a day fair enough?
- Ten dollars a day for seven days. I could earn enough for the trip! Thanks, Mom.
- So, can you start now?

B. GROUPS. Discuss these questions: What kind of work will Matt do to earn money for the trip? Would you help your parents in order to get some extra money?

Unit 7   69

8 I hadn't seen him in years.

1 Dialogue

B12 Cover the dialogue and listen.

Jack: Are we ready to go?
Scott: Hi, guys. Sorry I'm late. I met an old friend from Hawaii. I hadn't seen him in years. It was a real surprise.
Jack: That's OK. Is everybody here now?
Matt: Yes, so let's go.
Denise: You know what, Matt? I'm glad you're coming with us.
Matt: Really?
Denise: Really. I'm surprised, though. I didn't think Jack had invited you.
Jack: I didn't. He invited himself.
Denise: Matt, you can sit between Kelly and me in the back.
Jack: You just made his day, Denise.
(Later, at the park)
Matt: This is great. I hope we see some famous people here.
Denise: Who knows? Maybe we will.
Matt: Can we go to the Special Effects Stages first? And then can we go on the Jurassic Park ride? I heard it's really frightening.
Jack: Maybe. No promises. Let's check the map.
Kelly: Good idea!

Learning goals

Communication
Talk about a past incident

Grammar
The past perfect
The past perfect and the simple past

Vocabulary
Word building with verbs of emotion

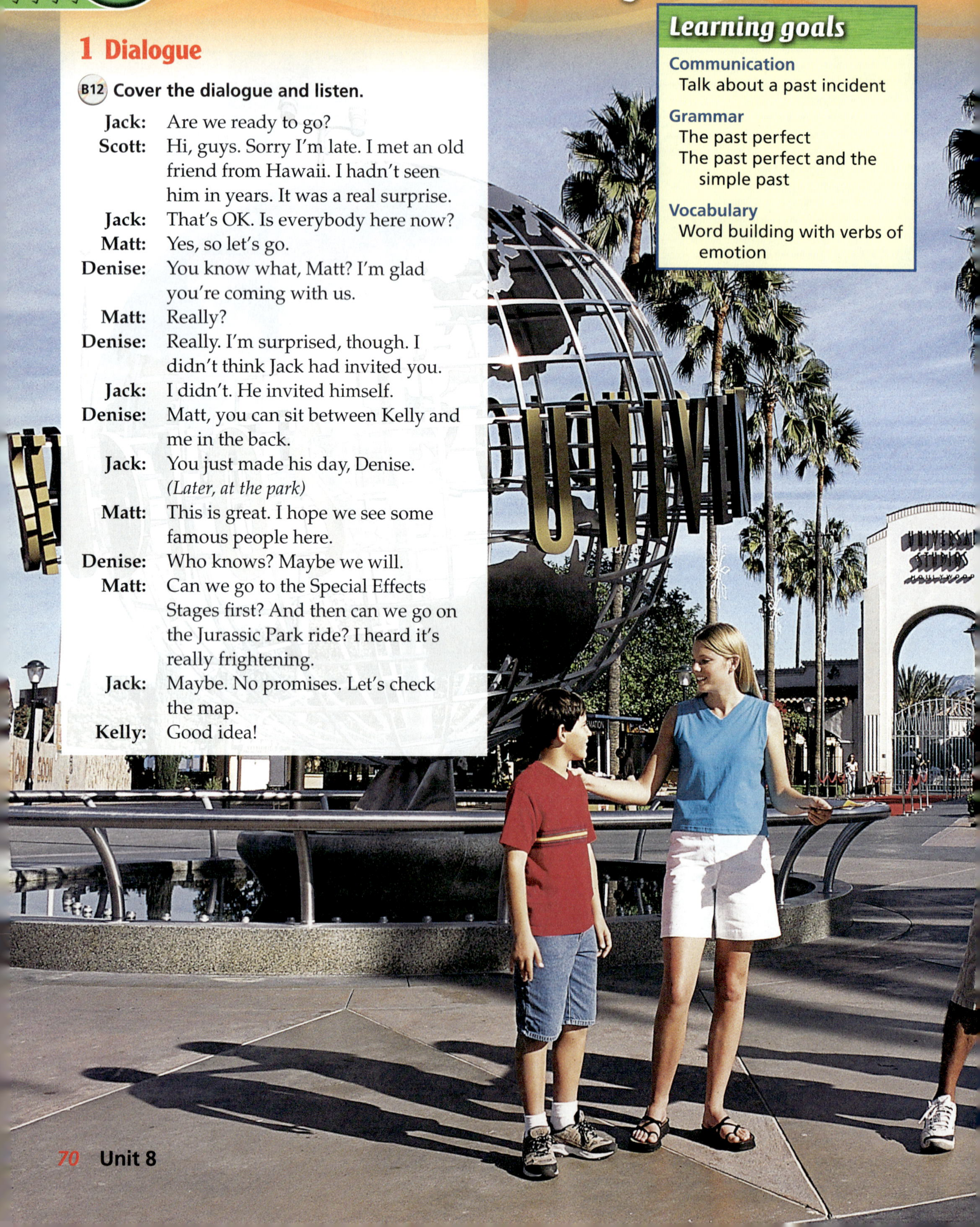

2 Comprehension

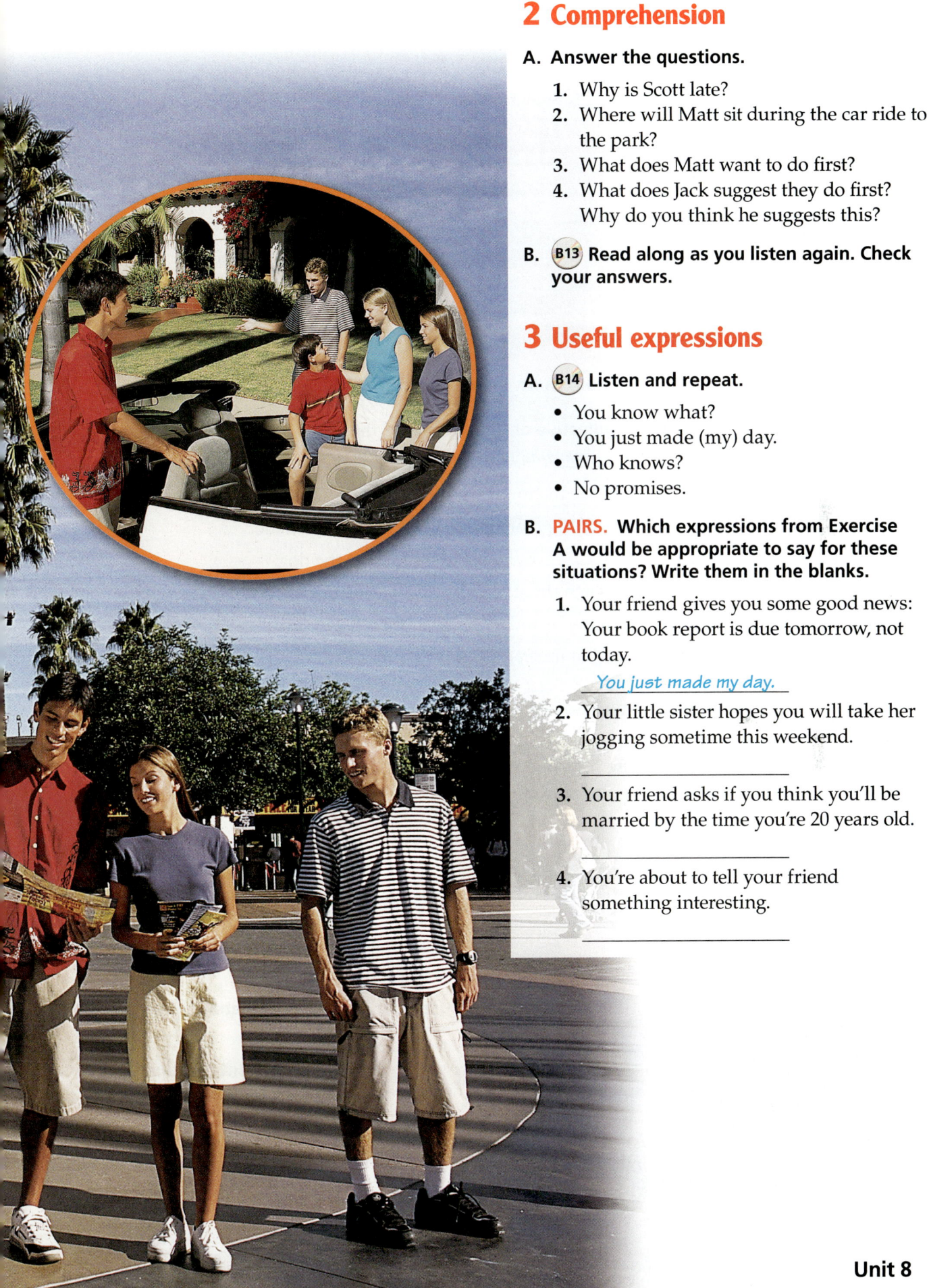

A. Answer the questions.

1. Why is Scott late?
2. Where will Matt sit during the car ride to the park?
3. What does Matt want to do first?
4. What does Jack suggest they do first? Why do you think he suggests this?

B. **B13** Read along as you listen again. Check your answers.

3 Useful expressions

A. **B14** Listen and repeat.
- You know what?
- You just made (my) day.
- Who knows?
- No promises.

B. **PAIRS.** Which expressions from Exercise A would be appropriate to say for these situations? Write them in the blanks.

1. Your friend gives you some good news: Your book report is due tomorrow, not today.
   You just made my day.

2. Your little sister hopes you will take her jogging sometime this weekend.
   _____

3. Your friend asks if you think you'll be married by the time you're 20 years old.
   _____

4. You're about to tell your friend something interesting.
   _____

Unit 8   71

4 Vocabulary

Word building with verbs of emotion

A. Complete the chart. You may use a dictionary.

Verb	Adjective with -ing	Adjective with -ed	Noun
1. to amaze	amazing	amazed	
2. to thrill			thrill
3. to surprise		surprised	
4. to excite			excitement
5. to shock	shocking		
6. to interest	interesting		
7. to frighten			fright

B. **B15** Listen and repeat the words in the chart. Check your answers.

C. Complete the sentences with the adjective or noun forms of the verbs in parentheses.

1. The light show was so (*amaze*) ____amazing____ that we couldn't believe our eyes.
2. It was a (*shock*) _____ to see the town after the hurricane hit.
3. I'm (*interest*) _____ in learning more about how movies are made.
4. The kitten was (*frighten*) _____ by the loud barking of the dog.
5. It was (*thrill*) _____ to watch the skiers race.
6. I didn't know about the party for my birthday. It was a (*surprise*) _____.
7. The roller-coaster ride was scary but (*excite*) _____.

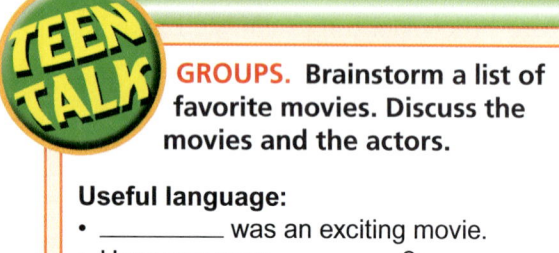

TEEN TALK

GROUPS. Brainstorm a list of favorite movies. Discuss the movies and the actors.

Useful language:
- _____ was an exciting movie.
- Have you seen _____?
- There were some amazing special effects.
- I was surprised by the ending. Were you?
- I love scary movies like _____.

5 Writing

A. Write notes about one of your favorite movies. Include the answers to these questions in your notes:

- What's one of your favorite movies?
- Who's in the movie?
- Think about the actors, the special effects, the story, and particular scenes (such as a car chase). Can you use any of the words in Exercise 4 to describe them?

B. Use your notes to write about your favorite movie.

C. **PAIRS.** Read and comment on your classmate's writing. Use the Peer editing checklist on page 134 to help you.

Grammar Focus

The past perfect

The movie started at 2:00 yesterday.

Affirmative statement:	Emmanuel arrived at 2:15. The movie **had started** by then.
Negative statement:	Douglas arrived at 1:45. The movie **hadn't started** by then.
Yes/No question:	**Had** the movie **started** by the time Teresa arrived?
Short answer:	Yes, it **had**. / No, it **hadn't**.

Some past perfect forms

come → had come	be → had been	have → had had
do → had done	get → had gotten	go → had gone
see → had seen	take → had taken	tell → had told

Discovering grammar

Look at the grammar chart. Circle the correct answers.

1. To make the past perfect form of a verb, use (*have* / *had*) + the past participle.
2. The answer to the question "Had you been there, before?" is ("*Yes, I did.*" / "*Yes, I had.*").

Practicing grammar

6 Practice

Fill in the blanks with the past perfect form of the verbs in parentheses.

1. Mark didn't want to come to the movie with us. He (*see*) ___had seen___ it twice.
2. The little girl (*learn*) _____ to read by her fourth birthday.
3. We were really hungry, because we (*not eat*) _____ before we left home.
4. Marlon started acting early. By the age of six, he (*perform*) _____ in many TV shows.
5. We got to the train station late. Fortunately, the train (*not leave*) _____ yet.

7 Practice

A. Read about Halle Berry's accomplishments. Then, in your notebook, write four more sentences like the one in the example.

For example:

By the time she was nineteen, she had won a beauty pageant.

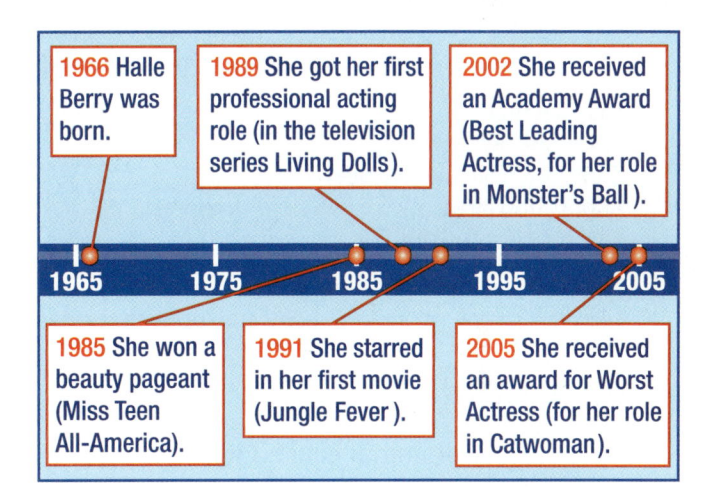

1966 Halle Berry was born.

1989 She got her first professional acting role (in the television series Living Dolls).

2002 She received an Academy Award (Best Leading Actress, for her role in Monster's Ball).

1965 1975 1985 1995 2005

1985 She won a beauty pageant (Miss Teen All-America).

1991 She starred in her first movie (Jungle Fever).

2005 She received an award for Worst Actress (for her role in Catwoman).

B. Use your sentences in Exercise A to write *Yes/No* questions in your notebook.

For example:

Had Halle Berry won a beauty pageant by the time she was nineteen?

C. PAIRS. Ask each other questions about the chart in Exercise A.

A: Had Halle Berry starred in a movie by the time she was twenty-one?

B: No, she hadn't.

Unit 8 73

8 Pronunciation

Reduction of function words

A. **B16** Function words (like *the*, *of*, *she*, and *had* in the past perfect) carry less meaning than content words. They also receive less stress. Listen.

She'd <u>seen</u> him <u>before</u>.

B. **B17** Underline the content words. Then listen and repeat the sentences. Give less stress to the function words.

1. They'd been to his soccer games.
2. He'd visited her school last year.
3. We'd eaten breakfast by 7:00.
4. She'd enjoyed her time at the car show.

9 Communication

Talk about a past incident

A. **B18** Listen and read.

A: Guess who I saw yesterday.
B: Who?
A: Bobby Carleton. Remember him? I almost didn't recognize him.
B: Really? Why?
A: Well, he'd changed a lot. He'd grown taller and he'd cut his hair.

B. **PAIRS.** Change the names in the conversation to people you know. Role-play the conversation.

GRAMMAR FOCUS

**The past perfect and the simple past:
Expressing the relationship between two past events**

Past perfect		Simple past
Dora **had** always **been** very shy	before	she **met** Danny.
Chris **had** never **seen** a bear	until	he **went** to Canada.
Angela **had** already **won** two singing contests	by the time	she **was** five years old
Alex **had** just **finished** his homework	when	someone **knocked** on the door.

The past perfect and adverbs
You can use *always*, *never*, *already*, and *just* with the past perfect.

Discovering grammar

Look at the grammar chart. Circle the correct answers.

1. When two past events relate to each other, use the past perfect for the (*earlier / later*) event.
2. When two past events relate to each other, use the simple past for the (*earlier / later*) event.

Practicing grammar

10 Practice

Fill in the blanks with the past perfect or the simple past forms of the verbs in parentheses.

1. Barbara (*just / open*) __had just opened__ the door when the phone (*ring*) __rang__.
2. My brothers (*eat*) _____ all the pizza by the time I (*get*) _____ home.
3. The people (*take*) _____ their seats by the time the play (*start*) _____.
4. My cat (*never / see*) _____ another cat until she (*see*) _____ herself in the mirror.
5. They (*just / got*) _____ off the ride when they (*start*) _____ to feel sick.

74 Unit 8

11 Practice

Read the following pairs of sentences. Write *1* before the sentence that happened first and *2* before the sentence that happened second. Then combine the sentences using the cues.

1. __2__ Rita asked me to fix her computer.
   __1__ Rita never spoke to me.
   Rita had never spoken to me until _she asked me to fix her computer_.

2. ____ We were at the airport for three hours.
   ____ My aunt's flight arrived.
   _____ by the time _____.

3. ____ Jake called Carmen four times.
   ____ Jake finally sent Carmen an e-mail.
   _____ before _____.

4. ____ My brother lost his wallet.
   ____ Mom gave my brother money.
   _____ before _____.

12 Practice

Have a competition! Go to page 132.

13 Listening

B19 Emily is talking to her friend Matthew. Listen. Then write *True* or *False*.

__True__ 1. Emily is writing a report on Albert Einstein.
_____ 2. Einstein had learned to speak by the time he was three.
_____ 3. Einstein was always a good student.
_____ 4. Einstein passed his first college entrance exam.
_____ 5. By age twenty-five, Einstein had obtained his doctorate.

14 Your turn

A. Choose from one of the following topics.

Find information about a person from history whom you admire.
OR
Find information about someone who was named *Time* magazine Person of the Year. You can find information about this on the Internet.

B. Write a short paragraph about the person you have chosen. Try to use the simple past and past perfect forms.

C. CLASS. Read your paragraph to the class.

Unit 8   75

Learn to learn

Make predictions.

Making predictions about what an article might be about will help you read with more understanding.

In Exercise 15, you will be reading about Albert Einstein. What do you imagine the article will talk about? Make some predictions and write them in your notebook or discuss them with a classmate.

For example:

The article might tell me about Einstein's life as a young man.

15 Reading

A. **B20** Read along silently as you listen.

Einstein: Person of the Century

He was a renowned scientist, a rebel, a genius, and a bumbling professor. Call him whatever you like, but this fact remains: Albert Einstein's genius changed our ideas of space and time and of the universe. To many, Einstein is the greatest scientist of all time. His relativity formula, $E = mc^2$, is one of the few scientific formulas that are familiar to nonscientists.

Einstein was born in 1879 in Ulm, Germany, and studied in Switzerland. By 1905, he had earned his doctorate, developed the theory of relativity, explained the photoelectric effect, and studied the movement of atoms. By 1909, his work had already attracted attention, and by 1913, Einstein had become famous. He received the Nobel Prize in Physics in 1921 for his work on the photoelectric effect.

When World War II broke out, the Nazi government took away Einstein's German citizenship because he was Jewish. By then, he had accepted a position at Princeton University in the United States, where he lived until his death in 1955.

Einstein believed in world peace. But in 1939, he wrote to President Franklin Roosevelt, warning him that the Germans might try to make an atom bomb. In response, Roosevelt encouraged research on atomic bombs. When American A-bombs were used to destroy Nagasaki and Hiroshima, Einstein expressed regret that he had played a role in the bomb's development. Before his death, he joined other scholars in a desperate plea for a ban on warfare.

Einstein was a genius, but he was also a simple and lovable man. He loved to play with children. He was never concerned with money. When he couldn't solve a problem, he would say in accented English, "Now I will a little tink." And he would walk back and forth thinking.

Today, we remember the little man in baggy pants and scraggly white hair as perhaps the most influential person of the last century and a person who still inspires us today. In fact, in January 2000, *Time* magazine named Albert Einstein the Person of the Twentieth Century.

B. **PAIRS.** Discuss these questions.

1. What predictions did you make about the article before you read it?
2. Did making predictions help you read with more understanding?

16 Comprehension

Answer the questions.

1. What had Einstein accomplished by age twenty-five?
2. What was Einstein's big regret?
3. What kind of person was Einstein?

Progress check Units 7 and 8

Test-taking tip: Don't get too nervous. Try to stay relaxed before and during your tests. Keep a positive attitude.

Grammar

A. Choose the correct verb forms. (3 points each)

1. If I ___ time, I'll call you tonight.
   a. have b. had c. have had *(a circled)*
2. If I ___ the answer, I would tell you.
   a. know b. will know c. knew
3. If Andrea ___ hard, she will pass the test.
   a. study b. will study c. studies
4. If I ___ you, I wouldn't stay up all night.
   a. am b. were c. will be

B. Read the sentences. Underline the events that happened first. (2 points each)

1. By the time Jack arrived, <u>everyone else had already left</u>.
2. When the alarm clock rang, I had just fallen asleep.
3. The game had already started when we got to the ballpark.
4. Before registration began, many students had decided what classes they wanted.
5. We had started the experiment when the fire alarm rang.

C. Complete each sentence with the past perfect form of the verb. (3 points each)

Finally, by 9 P.M., I (1. *finish*) __had finished__ my work, so I decided to go home. But by that time, most of the buses (2. *stop*) _____ running. I (3. *bring*) _____ a magazine, so at least I had something to read while I waited. Then I saw the bus go by, and I realized the driver (4. *forget*) _____ my stop. Luckily, I (5. *remember*) _____ to bring my cell phone. I tried to call my brother. Eventually, he answered. He (6. *fall*) _____ asleep in front of the TV.

Vocabulary

D. Complete the sentences. (3 points each)

1. That's (*interest*) __interesting__ news.
2. You gave me a (*shock*) _____, coming in so quietly!
3. Why are you (*surprise*) _____?
4. Being invited to join an Olympic team is a huge (*thrill*) _____.

E. Complete the sentences with the correct form of the verb phrase. (2 points each)

| go against | ~~go back on~~ | go for | go over |

1. Sam didn't want to __go back on__ his promise to take me for a ride.
2. Our Olympic team is _____ a gold medal.
3. Maria usually _____ her work twice before she gives it to the teacher.
4. If I were you, I wouldn't _____ your father's wishes.

Communication

F. PAIRS. Fill in the blanks. Then role-play the conversations. (5 points)

A: What would you do if someone gave you $1,000?
B: Hmm. I think _____.
A: Really? I wouldn't. I _____.

Now I can . . .
❑ talk about possible or imaginary situations.
❑ talk about wishes.
❑ talk about the relationship between two past events.

Unit 8 77

Game 3 Imagination

You need:
- a pencil
- a piece of paper

Steps:

1. Play this game in groups of three. Make a score sheet and write each player's name on it.

2. The first player asks a question based on the *if* clause in Frame 1.

   For example:

   S1: What would you do if you could see the future?

3. Going clockwise, the other two players each answer the question. The questioner gives a point to the player with the better answer (more creative and grammatically correct).

   For example:

   S2: If I could see the future, I'd never study for tests.
   S3: If I could see the future, I'd . . .

4. Going clockwise, the next player asks a question based on the *if* clause in Frame 2. The other two players each answer the question, and the questioner awards a point to the person with the better answer.

5. Continue with this pattern. At the end, the player with the most points wins.

Useful language
- Whose turn is it?
- I think your answer was better, so you get a point.

1. If I could see the future, . . .
2. If I had wings, . . .
3. If I found a big diamond ring on the street, . . .
4. If a genie gave me three wishes, . . .
5. If I were invisible, . . .
6. If my house were on fire and I could only save three things, . . .
7. If I found a big snake in my bed, . . .
8. If I could go back in time, . . .
9. If my parents were actually aliens from outer space, . . .

Project 3 — A snapshot of my ideal world

Describe an aspect of your ideal world. Use your imagination. Write a report about it. Use the steps below as a guide. Present your report to the class.

1. Choose a topic from the box.

   Schools
   Transportation
   Computers and the Internet
   Food and drink
   Health
   Houses
   Sports and entertainment
   Shopping
   My country
   The world

2. After you've chosen your topic, brainstorm how things will be in your ideal world of the future.

   Health Care in My Ideal World
   - no doctor visits
   - no hospitals
   - a computer chip under the skin will monitor health
   - laser surgery for everything
   - people will live longer and healthier lives

3. Write a first draft of your report.

4. Practice reading your report aloud in front of a classmate. Revise your report based on your classmate's suggestions. When you have finished revising it, transfer it onto note cards.

   Health

   In my ideal world, there will be no visits to doctors and hospitals. Everyone will have a little computer chip under the skin that will monitor his or her health. When a person becomes ill, the chip will send a signal to the central health computer system in the city where he or she lives. The computer will figure out what the problem is, and the person will immediately receive medication wherever he or she is. For a serious medical problem, a computerized laser surgery machine on wheels will come to the person's house and fix the problem in just a few minutes.

   The computer chip under the skin will also monitor if a person is eating, sleeping, and exercising well. People will save a lot of money on health care and will live much longer and healthier lives.

5. Present your report to the class. Use your notecards to help you.

9 Mom said I had to go.

1 Dialogue

B21 Cover the dialogue and listen.

Denise: What's wrong? Tell me it's not about Scott this time.
Kelly: It's not. I just got a call from my mom. She said she wanted me to go home next week.
Denise: Next week! Why?
Kelly: She said that I had to help her prepare for a family reunion.
Denise: A family reunion sounds like fun!
Kelly: Well, I'm not looking forward to it.
Denise: So what are you going to do?
Kelly: Go home, what else?
Denise: Have you told Scott yet?
Kelly: No. Not that he'd care.
Denise: Give him a break, Kelly. Maybe he does care.
Kelly: Maybe. Oh, by the way, Jack called. He asked if we wanted a ride to the surfing competition tomorrow. I told him we did. He'll pick us up around 9.

Learning goals

Communication
Report what someone has said

Grammar
Reported speech:
– Statements
– Questions
– Using *said* and *told*

Vocabulary
Idioms

2 Comprehension

A. **Answer the questions.**

1. How does Kelly feel about going home so soon?
2. What does Denise think of family reunions?
3. How do you know that Kelly is annoyed with Scott?
4. Where are Kelly and Denise going tomorrow?

B. (B22) **Read along as you listen again. Check your answers.**

3 Useful expressions

A. (B23) **Listen and repeat.**

- Next week!
- (Go home,) what else?
- Not that he'd care.
- (That) sounds like fun!

B. **Find a phrase that could follow each of these expressions. Write the letter.**

  _c_   1. Next week!   a. I'd enjoy that.
____ 2. Go home, what else?   b. I don't have any choice.
____ 3. Not that he'd care.   c. That's a surprise!
____ 4. That sounds like fun!   d. He's not interested.

4 Vocabulary

Idioms

A. (B24) **An idiom is a phrase that has a meaning different from the meaning of its individual parts. Listen and repeat the idioms below. Then match them with their meanings.**

  _c_   1. to look forward to   a. to hope for good results
____ 2. to give someone a break   b. to reach a decision
____ 3. to play it by ear   c. to expect with excitement
____ 4. to make up one's mind   d. to not keep one's promise
____ 5. to keep one's fingers crossed   e. to let someone have another chance
____ 6. to break one's word   f. to decide what to do as things happen

B. **Write sentences using the idioms in Exercise A. You may use any verb tense.**

1. _I'm looking forward to visiting Grandma during my vacation._
2. _____
3. _____
4. _____
5. _____
6. _____

Grammar Focus

Reported speech: Statements

Quoted speech	Reported speech
"I'm in 9th grade."	She said (that) she was in 9th grade.
"I want you to come home, Kelly."	She said (that) she wanted Kelly to come home.
"I'm not looking forward to it."	She said (that) she wasn't looking forward to it.
"I went to the party."	She said (that) she had gone to the party.
"I've seen the movie."	She said (that) she had seen the movie.
"I will study tonight."	She said (that) she would study tonight.
"I may take the train."	She said (that) she might take the train.
"I can do it."	She said (that) she could do it.

Discovering grammar

Look at the grammar chart. Complete the grammar rules using *simple past*, *past perfect*, or *past continuous*.

In reported speech, verbs often go one tense further back in the past. It works like this:

Quoted speech	Reported speech
If the verb is in the simple present,	it changes to the ___simple past___.
If the verb is in the simple past,	it changes to the _____.
If the verb is in the present perfect,	it changes to the _____.
If the verb is in the present continuous,	it changes to the _____.

Practicing grammar

5 Practice

Read what each person is saying. Rewrite their words as reported speech.

Alan: I don't want to go in because the water's too cold.

③ _____

Martin: I have too much to do!

① Martin said he had too much to do.

Benjie: I can't believe that I missed the game.

④ _____

Luis: My ice cream tastes awful!

② _____

Noel: I've passed my exams!

⑤ _____

82 Unit 9

6 Practice

Rewrite the sentences as reported speech.

1. She said, "I'm not on the right bus."
   <u>She said that she wasn't on the right bus.</u>

2. He said, "I picked her up at 6:00."
   _____

3. Dad said, "I won't get home early."
   _____

4. Grandma said, "We ate at a nice restaurant."
   _____

5. Mom said, "I need to get another job."
   _____

6. I said, "I don't understand the homework."
   _____

7 Practice

Have a competition! Go to page 132.

8 Pronunciation

Intonation in quoted and reported speech

A. **B25** Listen. First you will hear only the rhythm of the sentence. Then you will hear the sentence.

   She said, "I'm happy."
   She said she was happy.

B. **B26** Listen and repeat. Try to match the intonation you hear.

   1. She said, "I'm happy."
      She said she was happy.
   2. He said, "I live in Texas."
      He said he lived in Texas.
   3. She said, "I had a good time."
      She said she'd had a good time.
   4. He said, "I can run the fastest."
      He said he could run the fastest.

9 Communication

Report what someone has said

A. **B27** Listen and read.

   A: Hi, Dad.
   B: Hi, Robert. Hey, your cousin called while you were out.
   A: Miguel? What'd he say?
   B: He said he was leaving for the soccer field now. He said he'd meet you there.
   A: Good. But wait. Did he say which field he was going to?
   B: Uh, no. I don't think he did.
   A: Hmm. OK. I'll call his cell.

B. **PAIRS.** Role-play the phone conversation that Robert's dad had with Miguel. Start like this:

   Dad: Hello.
   Miguel: Hi, Mr. Lopez. Is Robert there?

TEEN TALK

GROUPS. Talk about how you use the phone. Ask and answer questions.
- How often do you talk on your cell phone?
- When do you text? When do you talk in person?
- Do you ever leave a voice message?
- Give me an example of a message you left recently.

Unit 9   83

Grammar Focus

Reported speech: Questions

Yes/No questions

Quoted speech	Reported speech
"**Do** you **want** a ride to the surfing competition?"	Jack asked (them) if they **wanted** a ride to the surfing competition.
"**Have** you **told** Scott?"	Denise asked (her) if she **had told** Scott.
"**Will** you **be** home tonight?"	He asked (me) if I **would be** home tonight.
"**Are** you **free** next Saturday?"	He asked (me) if I **was free** next Saturday.
"**Have** you **been** studying a lot?"	He asked (me) if I **had been** studying a lot.
"**Can** we **study** together?"	He asked (me) if we **could study** together.

Information questions

Quoted speech	Reported speech
"What**'s** your new job?"	He asked (me) what my new job **was**.
"When **are** your days off?"	He asked (me) when my days off **were**.
"When **did** you **start** working?"	He asked (me) when I **had started** working.
"Why **do** you **like** your job?"	He asked (me) why I **liked** my job.

Discovering grammar

Look at the grammar chart. Which is correct, a or b? Check (✔) your answer.

1. ❏ a. I asked him that he would help me.
   ❏ b. I asked him if he would help me.
2. ❏ a. I asked her what her name was.
   ❏ b. I asked her what was her name.
3. ❏ a. She asked me where had I been.
   ❏ b. She asked me where I had been.

Practicing grammar

10 Practice

Billy is asking Judy, a new student, some questions. Rewrite Billy's questions as reported speech.

1. "Are you a new student?"
   He asked her if she was a new student.

2. "When did you move to the neighborhood?"
   _____

3. "What do you think of the school?"
   _____

4. "Have you met all your teachers?"
   _____

5. "Have you been able to find everything OK?"
   _____

11 Listening

A. **B28** Listen to Rob's message. Then write his questions. Use the cues.

1. "Are *you nervous about our math exam?*"
2. "Can _____
3. "Will _____
4. "What _____
5. "Have _____
6. "Where _____

B. Write the questions in Exercise A as reported speech.

1. *Rob asked Mara if she was nervous about their math exam.*
2. _____
3. _____
4. _____
5. _____
6. _____

GRAMMAR FOCUS

Reported speech: Using *said* and *told*

Kenji **said** (to Serena) that he was leaving.
Kenji **told Serena/her** that he was leaving.

Lisette **said** (to her brother) that he was getting taller.
Lisette **told her brother/him** that he was getting taller.

Discovering grammar

Look at the grammar chart. Circle the correct answer.

In reported speech, (*told* / *said*) is always followed immediately by a noun or an object pronoun.

Practicing grammar

12 Practice

Complete each sentence with a form of *say* or *tell*.

1. Tracy ___told___ me she liked the brown hat.
   I _____ her the yellow one was cuter.
2. Liz _____ it wasn't going to rain on Saturday.
   John _____ he was keeping his fingers crossed.
3. José _____ us the new Prince CD was great.
   He _____ we should all buy it.
4. Donna _____ she loved sushi.
   Ray _____ Donna he had never tried sushi before.
5. Dad _____ Timmy to help his brother wash the car.
   Timmy _____ he would be there in a minute.

13 Practice

Rewrite the sentences below as reported speech. Use the cues.

1. Dan (to Lisa): "I'm preparing dinner."
   (told) _Dan told Lisa he was preparing dinner._
   (said) _Dan said he was preparing dinner._
2. Carmen (to Ben): "You need a vacation."
   (told) _____
   (said) _____
3. Andrea (to Mr. Galindo): "I may not be able to finish the project on time."
   (told) _____
   (said) _____
4. Karen (to her aunt): "You look great!"
   (told) _____
   (said) _____
5. Antony (to Susan): "I'm going to Hawaii!"
   (told) _____
   (said) _____

Unit 9   85

14 Reading

A. Before you read, look up the meanings of the underlined words.

B. **B29** Read along silently as you listen.

FAMILY REUNIONS

Some people dread family reunions because they hate facing endless questions and scrutiny from relatives. Others look forward to them as a chance to show off their successes. But family reunions allow many people to reconnect with their past and to discover their own identities. "Knowing where you come from gives you a little head start on where you're going," says an editor of *Reunions* magazine. A woman who has just attended a three-day family gathering agrees: "You are who your relatives were. You can't understand what's happening in the present if you don't understand what has happened in the past."

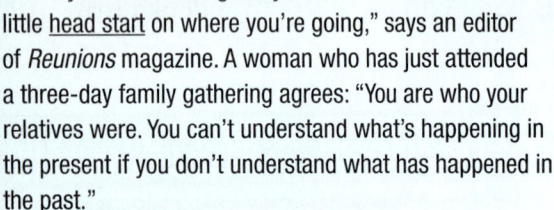

Family reunions have always enabled splintered families to re-establish ties. But they are more necessary—and emotional—than ever now, because many of today's family members are separated not only by miles but also by continents and oceans. "We are more emotionally connected to members of our family than we are to our neighbors," says a sociologist. He adds that we need our families to approve of our lives and our life choices. In other words, the most important source of acceptance and approval of what we have become is the family.

Of course, the rituals and activities at family reunions have changed over the years. We live in an entertainment-hungry culture. We are no longer content with big family dinners, where family members talk and laugh about the old days or gush over each other's children. Today's family reunions are hectic and complicated events. Some are held in resorts and hotels with preplanned tours, games, and other activities. Things can get so stressful that after the event, people sometimes realize that they have forgotten to say hello to a cousin or an aunt and uncle. But then there's always the next family reunion!

15 Comprehension

Answer the questions.

1. Why do many people like going to family reunions?
2. Why do some people dislike going to family reunions?

16 Writing

A. **GROUPS.** Discuss these questions.

1. Have you ever been to a family reunion? What was it like?
2. Do you enjoy family reunions? What do you like about them? What don't you like about them?
3. Imagine your family has a reunion. Describe it.

B. Choose one of the topics you discussed in Exercise A. Write a paragraph in your notebook.

Learn to learn

Keep a vocabulary notebook.

- You can build your vocabulary by writing new, useful words in a vocabulary notebook.

You may already have a vocabulary notebook. If not, start one now. Include the underlined words from Exercise 14. Specify the part of speech, and give sample sentences whenever possible.

For example:

dread (v.) to dread is to feel very worried about something. (n.) the feeling of dread.
Example: I feel dread when I go into an exam room.

Putting it together Walking with Scott

A. B30 **Listen and read. What does Kelly tell Scott twice?**

1. **Kelly:** Are you worried about tomorrow's competition, Scott?
   Scott: Me, worried? Of course not. I'm all set. My trainer told me I should win easily.

2. **Kelly:** And you believe him?
   Scott: Why not? He said I was one of the best in the competition.

3. **Kelly:** Um, Scott? I'm leaving a week from now.
   Scott: Uh-huh.

4. **Kelly:** Did you hear what I just said? I said I was leaving next week.
   Scott: Yeah, I heard you. You need a ride to the airport or something?
   Kelly: No. So, what are you going to do after the competition?
   Scott: I'm going to play it by ear. I might go to Florida with some of the surfers.

5. **Kelly:** I see. Well, it's getting late. I'd better head home.
   Scott: OK. I think I'll hang out here for a while. Are you going to watch me compete tomorrow?

6. **Kelly:** It's always about you, isn't it? You're not the center of the universe, you know.
   Scott: Huh? What did I say?

B. **GROUPS.** **Discuss these questions:** Why is Kelly angry with Scott? Should she be angry with him?

Unit 9 87

Wide Angle on the world

1 Reading

Reading skill: Reading for Who, What, Why
When you read articles, ask yourself questions such as Who (or What) is this about? Why is it important? Answering these questions will help you understand the main ideas.

A. Read the questions. Then read the article, keeping these questions in mind as you read.

1. Stephanie Lefeldt
   a. Why did Stephanie start her group?
   b. Why does Stephanie's group want people to try weaving on a loom?
2. Ram Bopalakrishnan
   a. Who did Ram and his friends start a school for?
   b. How does Ram's group get students to return to class?

B. **PAIRS.** Take turns asking and answering the questions in Exercise A.

2 Listening

B31 Listen. Check the things that Elizabeth has done at her local homeless shelter.

- ❏ cleaned
- ❏ collected supplies
- ❏ cooked meals
- ❏ created a garden
- ❏ created a library
- ❏ created a playroom
- ❏ helped build the shelter
- ❏ provided food

3 Speaking

GROUPS. Discuss the following:

Choose one of the issues below. Imagine your group is an organization that helps people with this issue. Talk about why the issue is important and what your group can do to help.

care for the elderly	school dropouts
homelessness	teen drug use
relationship problems	teen smoking

4 Writing

You want to create an action group that will help address the issue you chose in Exercise 3. Write plans for your group. Include details such as who your plan will help and what you might do.

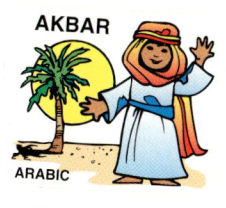

TAKING ACTION

...GERMANY

...the more than 250 million child workers in the world. She says ...g children. They don't get to play tag, skip rope, or dream. When ...ntry was importing Asian carpets made by young children, she ...n in the Carpet Industry. The group's goal is to prevent human ...en, especially child laborers in the carpet industry. The group talks ...educate them about the situation and to tell them how they can ...up's projects is creating a "weaving loom." They plan to display the ...ores. They want shoppers to try it so they can see how hard a child ...ust one carpet.

...ALAKRISHNAN, 16, INDIA

...problem in India, so Ram, ...ome friends, started a free ...underprivileged children in his ...ood. The thirty students meet ...rage. According to Ram, girls ...opportunities in education ...do, so he makes a special effort ...girls in his classes. Ram's group ...ree books and other school ...Dropout rates are high in India, ...up gives cookies to the students ...d of the day to encourage them ...back. Ram plans to introduce a ...amination system so students will ...studies seriously.

Wide Angle 3   89

10 He's not good enough to win.

1 Dialogue

B32 **Cover the dialogue and listen.**

Scott: Hi, guys. I'm glad you're here, Kelly. You told me you weren't coming.
Kelly: I didn't say I wasn't coming.
Scott: Well, not directly. It doesn't matter. The important thing is you're all here to watch me compete!
Kelly: Wow. Look at those waves. They look so powerful.
Scott: Yeah, but I'm strong enough to handle them.
Kelly: Yeah. You're too good to fall, aren't you, Scott?
Scott: I'm, uh, . . . well, I've got to run. Cheer for me, Kelly, OK?

Jack: Look at him! He's such a show-off.
Denise: Do you think he'll win, Jack?
Jack: I don't think he's good enough to win, but who knows?
Denise: There's Kenji, over there. He's a fantastic surfer.

Denise: Hey, see that huge wave over there? It's coming toward Scott and Kenji.
Jack: Whoa! That *is* big! Let's see Scott handle that one.
Denise: Kenji's doing great! He looks awesome!
Jack: Uh-oh. Where's Scott?
Kelly: He's over there, hanging on to his surfboard! He wiped out!

Learning goals

Communication
Express disappointment

Grammar
Too + adjective/adverb + *to*;
 (*not*) adjective/adverb + *enough* + *to*
So + a clause of result
Such + a clause of result

Vocabulary
Strong adjectives

90 Unit 10

2 Comprehension

A. Answer the questions.

1. How do you think Scott feels when he sees Kelly?
2. According to Jack, what are Scott's chances of winning?
3. What happened to Scott in the competition?
4. Which line in the dialogue shows Scott is confident he will do well?

B. (B33) Read along as you listen again. Check your answers.

3 Useful expressions

A. (B34) Listen and repeat. Then match the expressions that have similar meanings.

__c__ 1. It doesn't matter.   a. I have to go.

____ 2. I'm glad you're here.   b. It's difficult to say.

____ 3. Who knows?   c. It's not important.

____ 4. I've got to run.   d. I'm happy you came.

B. **PAIRS.** Write two short conversations. Use one of the expressions in each conversation. Then role-play your conversations.

4 Vocabulary

Strong adjectives

A. (B35) Strong adjectives are used to express strong emotions. Listen and repeat.

- devastated
- ecstatic
- exhausted
- fantastic
- huge
- terrible
- terrified
- tiny

B. Next to each adjective below, write the corresponding strong adjective. Choose from the list in Exercise A.

1. small __tiny__   5. afraid _____
2. big _____   6. happy _____
3. tired _____   7. bad _____
4. good _____   8. disappointed _____

5 Practice

Have a competition! Go to page 133.

Unit 10

GRAMMAR FOCUS

Too + adjective/adverb + to;
(not) adjective/adverb + enough + to

You're **too good to fall**.
He's driving **too slowly to get there** in time.

He's **not good enough to win**.
I'm **strong enough to handle** the waves.
She's **not** running **fast enough to break** the record.

Discovering grammar

Look at the grammar chart. Circle the correct answers.

1. *Too* comes (*before* / *after*) the adjective or adverb.
2. *Enough* comes (*before* / *after*) the adjective or adverb.

Practicing grammar

6 Practice

Unscramble the words to write sentences.

1. big / John isn't / to be on the team / enough
   John isn't big enough to be on the team.

2. too / It's not / to order breakfast / late
   _____

3. Tommy is / terrified / to sleep without a light on / too
   _____

4. enough / The dog is barking / to wake the whole neighborhood / loudly
   _____

5. to win the race / too / Larry is running / slowly
   _____

6. Kathy isn't / to go on the rollercoaster / enough / tall
   _____

7 Practice

Complete the sentences with *too* or *enough* and the adjectives in parentheses.

1. The children have to play inside today. The weather isn't (*warm*) __*warm enough*__ to play outside.

2. No, you're not (*old*) _____ to go to parties without an adult.

3. I think she's (*young*) _____ to wear makeup.

4. Can you turn up the volume? It's (*soft*) _____ to hear.

5. My teacher thinks that some kids aren't (*responsible*) _____ to use the Internet without supervision.

6. Three miles! That's (*far*) _____ to walk!

7. It's only 11:00. It's (*early*) _____ to have lunch.

8. My MP3 plays isn't (*tiny*) _____ to fit in my pocket.

8 Practice

Combine the sentences. Add *too* or *enough*.

1. Kenji is very talented. He'll win the surfing competition.
   Kenji is talented enough to win the surfing competition.

2. This car is really big. It won't fit in that parking space.
   _____

3. I'm tired. I can't stay up late for the movie.
   _____

4. She's smart. She might get a scholarship.
   _____

9 Listening

B36 Listen and complete the sentences with the correct information.

1. Kenji may be ___*good enough*___ to win.
2. Mark's _____ to compete.
3. Sheila's _____ to compete.
4. Sara's _____ to compete.
5. Scott's probably not _____ to win.

10 Your Turn

A. Think about your classmates and other friends in school. Create a sentence about someone using this pattern:

_____ is | talented / smart / tall / funny / (*your idea*) | enough to be _____.

B. GROUPS. Read your sentences to each other and respond.

For example:

A: Felipe is funny enough to be on a comedy show.
B: You're right, he is.

11 Writing

A. Fill in the chart below. Check (✓) whether you are old enough or not old enough to do each of the following activities. Add two tasks of your own.

TASK	Old enough	Not old enough
Drive a car		
Have a job		
Baby-sit		
Make dinner		
Have an ATM card		

B. In your notebook, write about something you're not old enough to do yet. Describe what you'll do when you're old enough to do it.

For example:

> I'm not old enough to drive a car. But I love cars, and I think driving will be fun. When I'm old enough to drive, I'll drive my friends home from school every day . . .

TEEN TALK

Talk about things you look forward to doing when you're older.

Useful language:
- I look forward to . . .
- I can't wait until I can . . .
- I'm planning to . . . when I'm older.
- I feel/don't feel the same way about that.

GRAMMAR FOCUS

So + a clause of result

The waves were powerful. Scott fell off his surfboard.
The waves were **so powerful** that Scott fell off his surfboard.

San Diego is pretty. Everyone wants to live there.
San Diego is **so pretty** that everyone wants to live there.

Discovering grammar

Look at the grammar chart. Complete the grammar rules.

1. Use _____ to add emphasis to an adjective.
2. Use _____ to connect two sentences.

Practicing grammar

12 Practice

Add *so* for emphasis. Then connect the sentences.

1. The tea is hot. I can't drink it.
   The tea is so hot that I can't drink it.
2. My brother is smart. He hardly ever has to study.
   _____
3. The tickets are expensive. I can't afford to buy them.
   _____
4. We were hungry. We couldn't wait for you to arrive before we ate.
   _____
5. Buenos Aires is beautiful. Its nickname is "The Paris of South America."
   _____

13 Practice

A. PAIRS. Complete the sentences with a clause of result. Say your sentences aloud to your classmate.

1. I was so tired . . .
2. My shoes are so old . . .
3. It was so hot outside . . .
4. They were making so much noise . . .
5. The soccer game went on for so long . . .
6. (*make your own sentence*)

B. GROUPS. Take turns reporting what your classmate said.

A: Felipe said he was so tired that he couldn't keep his eyes open.
B: Barbara said they were making so much noise in the courtyard that she had to close the classroom windows.

GRAMMAR FOCUS

Such + a clause of result

There were powerful waves. Scott fell off his surfboard.
There were **such powerful waves** that Scott fell off his surfboard.

San Diego is a pretty city. Everyone wants to live there.
San Diego is **such a pretty city** that everyone wants to live there.

Discovering grammar

Look at the examples in the grammar chart. Circle the correct answers.

1. Use (*so* / *such*) to describe an adjective alone.
2. Use (*so* / *such*) to describe an adjective followed by a noun.

Practicing grammar

14 Practice

Combine the sentences. Add *such*.

1. It was a good movie. I want to see it again.
   It was such a good movie that I want to see it again.

2. Those are popular toys. All the stores are sold out of them.

3. These are expensive shoes. I can't afford to buy them.

4. Italy is an interesting country. We never go anywhere else for vacation.

5. It was a huge pizza. We weren't able to eat all of it.

15 Practice

Complete each sentence with *so* or *such*, plus the adjective in parentheses. Add the article *a* or *an* if needed. Put the verb in the result clause into the correct tense.

1. It was (lovely) *such a lovely* day that we (go) *went* on a picnic.
2. I'm (happy) _____ in this class that I (not want) _____ it to end!
3. The museum was (crowded) _____ that we (find) _____ it difficult to see the paintings.
4. My sister was (mad) _____ at me that she (hang up) _____ the phone.
5. It is (long) _____ drive that we always (fly) _____ there instead.
6. He's (lazy) _____ that he never (finish) _____ his homework.
7. You're speaking in (loud) _____ voice that everyone (look) _____ at us.

16 Pronunciation

Emphatic stress with *so* and *such*

A. **B37** Listen.

so pretty / Paris is so pretty.
such a pretty city / Paris is such a pretty city.

B. **B38** Listen and repeat.

1. Scott is so exhausted.
2. The waves were so huge.
3. Kelly is so angry at Scott.
4. It was such a great competition.
5. There were such long lines to get in.
6. San Diego has such beautiful beaches.

17 Communication

Express disappointment

A. **B39** Listen and read.

A: So what happened out there tonight?
B: Who knows? We were so close to winning that I could almost taste it!
A: I know. But you played well. And you did your best.
B: Yeah. But they were such a tough team.
A: They were. But there's always next time, right?
B: Yeah, I guess.

B. **PAIRS.** Create a conversation like the one in Exercise A. Include *so* and *such*. Role-play your conversation in front of another pair.

Unit 10 95

18 Reading

A. Before you read, look up the meanings of the underlined words in the article below. Then, in your notebook, write down a synonym (a word with a similar meaning) or a paraphrase (a phrase with a similar meaning) for each underlined word.

B. B40 Read along silently as you listen.

THE ISLANDS OF ALOHA

Picture this: sparkling white beaches, blue waters, colorful tropical flowers, palm trees, and warm sunshine. Hawaii is almost too beautiful to describe. To get a real sense of Hawaii's breathtaking beauty, you have to experience it for yourself.

Hawaii is made up of numerous islands. Four of the biggest ones are Oahu, Molokai, Maui, and Big Island (Hawaii). Each of these islands has its own particular charms.

Oahu is home to Honolulu, the cosmopolitan capital of Hawaii. Honolulu is great for shopping and going out, but for surfers, the lures of Waikiki are too powerful to ignore. The waves that break at world-famous Waikiki Beach are ideal for surfing.

If you prefer relaxation to excitement, Molokai is the place for you. People come to this island to unwind and to enjoy the simple life. Don't look for McDonald's or a movie theater here. This island is so simple and small that it doesn't even have traffic lights.

It is said that no matter where you go on Maui, you're bound to see rainbows. Maui is such a beautiful place that it was labeled the "Best Island in the World" by a popular travel magazine. Maui boasts countless waterfalls and the world's largest dormant volcano, Haleakala. People love to hike to the summit of Haleakala and watch the sun rise above the clouds.

Hiking, cycling, or riding horseback are the best ways to experience the Big Island's amazing natural wonders. One of the most famous of these wonders is Kilauea, the largest active volcano in the world. It's an amazing sight—but if you decide to hike to the summit, make sure you don't get too close to the red-hot lava spewing out of its craters!

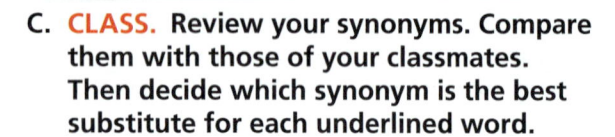

C. CLASS. Review your synonyms. Compare them with those of your classmates. Then decide which synonym is the best substitute for each underlined word.

19 Comprehension

Answer the questions.

1. What does each of the following Hawaiian islands have to offer?
   a. Oahu   c. Maui
   b. Big Island d. Molokai
2. What is the difference between the famous Hawaiian volcanoes Haleakala and Kilauea?

20 Speaking

GROUPS. Which of the Hawaiian islands would you most like to visit? Give reasons for your answer.

Learn to learn

Find the right word.

Sometimes you want to express an idea but you don't know the exact words you need. Your teacher or one of your classmates will usually be able to help you figure out the right words, if you know how to ask.

PAIRS. Practice the conversation with a classmate.

A: What's another word for "shining"? You use it when you talk about sand, or clear water in the sunlight.
B: Do you mean "sparkling"?
A: Yes, that's it. Thanks.

Tip: Try using the phrases that you learned in Exercise A soon, so you don't forget how to use them.

Progress check — Units 9 and 10

> **Test-taking tip:** Don't make assumptions.
> This is a common error in test taking. Always read a question carefully. Don't make assumptions about what the question might be.

Grammar

A. Write the sentences with *too* or *enough*. Use the cues. (3 points each)

1. I / fit / run eight laps around the track (*not enough*)
   I'm not fit enough to run eight laps around the track.

2. This exercise / difficult / do without a dictionary (*too*)
   _____

3. My brother / old / stay at home on his own (*not enough*)
   _____

4. Some bugs / tiny / see without a microscope (*too*)
   _____

B. Read Andrea's journal entry. Fill in the blanks with *so* or *such a/an*. (3 points each)

Dear Journal,

I did (1) *such an* embarrassing thing today! I was at the beach with Jenna. We were buying lemonade at the snack bar.

It was (2) _____ hot that we bought extra-large sizes. When I turned around to leave, this guy that I like, Andrew, was right behind me! I was (3) _____ surprised to see him that I dropped my drink . . . right on his feet! What a nightmare! He wasn't mad at me, though. In fact, he's (4) _____ nice guy that he offered to buy me a new drink. But I was (5) _____ embarrassed that I ran out of the snack bar without even saying I'm sorry. I can't believe I did that!

Vocabulary

C. Complete the sentences with the idioms from the box. Use the correct form of the verbs. (3 points each)

~~break your word~~	give her a break
look forward to	make up her mind
play it by ear	

1. You never keep your promises. You're always *breaking your word*.
2. I love summer. I always _____ it.
3. She _____. She decided to take guitar lessons instead of piano lessons.
4. We haven't made any definite plans for today. We're going to _____.
5. Will you _____? She's really doing her best.

Communication

D. Put the conversation in order. Then role-play the conversation. (3 points each)

___ It wasn't so tough! I can't believe this. We can't win without Ramón.

___ You're kidding! Did he say why not?

___ I guess it isn't. But it sure is nice.

_1_ Ramón called. He said he couldn't come to the game today.

___ He told me he was too exhausted to do anything. He said your track practice yesterday was really tough.

___ Oh, well. Winning isn't everything.

> **Now I can . . .**
> ❏ quote exactly what someone said.
> ❏ report what someone said.
> ❏ express disappointment

Unit 10 97

11 Solutions were discussed.

1 Reading

B41 Read along silently as you listen.

The State of the Planet

In 1992, the first Earth Summit meeting was held to discuss the state of the environment. World leaders from over 100 countries gathered in Rio de Janeiro to talk about the state of the environment. At that meeting, speeches were made, various solutions to preserve the environment were discussed, and agreements were signed.

Since then, meetings have been held every five years to monitor how well countries are responding to the challenge of the Rio Summit. How are we doing? There is some good news. Population growth is slowing down, and the hole in the ozone layer has begun to shrink. But some big problems remain. The earth's climate and biodiversity are still threatened, and food and water supplies remain tight, especially in poorer countries.

The map below shows the earth's environmental problems and some of its trouble spots.

Learning goals

Communication
Ask for information by telephone

Grammar
The passive voice

Vocabulary
Environmental issues
The natural environment

CARBON EMISSIONS
Most of the world's greenhouse gases are produced by the United States, Russia, and China. Countries that cannot afford high-tech solutions are likely to suffer the most from the effects of greenhouse gases.

DEFORESTATION
In the Amazon region, forests covering thousands of square miles are destroyed every year to create new farmland. If this is not regulated, planet Earth will lose many of its rainforests.

THINNING ICE
Ice in the arctic region is melting because of global warming. This could lead to rising sea levels and severe storms and droughts.

DROUGHT
Food and water shortages are caused by long periods with no rain. People in southern Africa are constantly threatened by hunger because of droughts.

ANTARCTIC WARMING
The Antarctic Peninsula has experienced a warming of about 4.5 degrees Fahrenheit (2.5 degrees Celsius) since the 1940s.

2 Comprehension

Answer the questions.

1. Why did world leaders meet at the 1992 Earth Summit in Rio de Janeiro?
2. What positive news is there about the environment?
3. What major problems have remained unsolved since the Summit?
4. What other environmental problems does the earth continue to face?

3 Vocabulary

Environmental issues

A. B42 Listen and repeat.

biodiversity	carbon emission
climate	coral reef
deforestation	~~drought~~
global warming	ozone layer

B. Match the definitions with the words and phrases in Exercise A.

1. A long period of dry weather when there is not enough water. ____drought____
2. The layer of gases that prevents the sun's harmful radiation from reaching Earth. _____
3. A rocklike formation near the surface of the sea made by tiny sea creatures. _____
4. The process of the clearing of forests. _____
5. The gradual rising of temperatures all over the planet. _____
6. The typical weather conditions in a particular area. _____
7. Variety in the number of species of plants and animals. _____
8. The sending out of poisonous gas when engines burn gasoline. _____

THREATENED REEFS

Indonesia's coral reefs, home to thousands of marine species, are severely damaged by overfishing and pollution.

Map Key

- Evergreen forest
- Deforestation in the Amazon
- Urban areas with more than 10 million people
- Highly threatened coral reefs
- Highly polluted areas

Unit 11   99

GRAMMAR FOCUS

The passive voice: Statements

Simple present
Forests **are destroyed** to create farmland.
People in southern Africa **are threatened** by hunger.

Simple past
The first Earth Summit meeting **was held** in Rio de Janeiro.
Speeches **were made** and agreements **were signed**.

Discovering grammar

Look at the grammar chart. Circle the correct answers.

1. We often use the passive voice when the doer of the action is (*not important* / *important*).
2. To form the passive, use a form of *be* + the (*past participle* / *present participle*).
3. Use the word (*from* / *by*) with a noun if it is important to show who or what the doer of the action is.

Practicing grammar

4 Practice

PAIRS. Rewrite each of the signs shown on the right as complete sentences. Use the simple present passive voice.

1. *Smoking is not allowed.*
2. _____
3. _____
4. _____
5. _____
6. _____
7. _____

5 Practice

Complete the sentences with the verbs in parentheses. Use the simple past passive voice.

When the United States (1. *hit*) __was hit__ by Hurricane Katrina in the summer of 2005, many young people came forward and made a difference.

Their first aim was to help the people who (2. *leave*) _____ homeless by the hurricane. In the spring of 2006, a number of young people (3. *persuade*) _____ to give up their Spring Break plans in order to volunteer as construction workers. They (4. *send*) _____ to the area by organizations like *Habitat for Humanity*. These young people (5. *credit*) _____ with helping many families start to rebuild their lives. Grateful families now live in homes that (6. *build*) _____ by young volunteers.

Signs:
- No Smoking
- Bicycles and skateboards not allowed in this area
- Volunteers Wanted
- Bathing suits required in swimming pools
- ID REQUIRED BEFORE ENTRY
- No Littering
- No camping allowed beyond this point

6 Dialogue

B43 Cover the dialogue and listen.

Jack: I can't believe you're leaving soon. Are you needed at home?
Kelly: Yeah, we're having a family reunion and I have to be there.
Denise: Did you tell Scott? What's going on between you two these days?
Kelly: Scott who?
Jack: Yeah, forget him. Guess what! I've joined TIG.
Denise: What's that?
Jack: It stands for Taking It Global. It's a volunteer group. They have a lot of projects to help save the environment. I'm joining the Beach Cleanup team.
Denise: And you're telling us this because . . . ?
Jack: Well, I was asked to find more volunteers. Do you want to volunteer this weekend? It should be fun.
Denise: You think cleaning the beach is fun?
Jack: Come on, Denise. You should help out.
Kelly: Yeah, Denise. Let's help.
Denise: Oh, all right.

7 Comprehension

A. Answer the questions.
 1. How does Kelly feel about Scott now?
 2. What is TIG?
 3. What does Jack ask the girls to do?

B. **B44** Read along as you listen again. Check your answers.

8 Useful expressions

A. **B45** Listen and repeat.
 1. What's going on between (you and David)?
 2. Forget (him).
 3. Guess what!
 4. And you're telling (me) this because . . . ?

B. Match each expression in Exercise A with a phrase that has the same meaning.

 __2__ a. Don't think about him anymore.
 ____ b. Why are you telling me this?
 ____ c. I have news for you.
 ____ d. How's your relationship with David?

GRAMMAR FOCUS

The passive voice: Questions

Yes/No questions
Are you **needed** at home?
Was Jack **asked** to find more volunteers?
Were the surfers **told** to help?

Short answers
Yes, I **am**./No, I**'m not**.
Yes, he **was**./No, he **wasn't**.
Yes, they **were**./No, they **weren't**.

Information questions
When **are** the volunteers **expected** to arrive?
Why **were** they **asked** to bring friends?

Short answers
Saturday morning.
Because there's a lot of work to do.

Discovering grammar

Look at the grammar chart. Circle the correct answers.

1. Use the (*base* / *past participle*) form of the main verb in passive voice questions.
2. (*Use* / *Don't use*) the main verb in short answers.

Practicing grammar

9 Practice

Rewrite the sentences as *yes* or *no* questions.

1. The students were asked to help with the cleanup.
   Were the students asked to help with the cleanup?
2. Spanish is spoken in many countries.
   _____
3. The school was built in 1990.
   _____
4. The bank is open only on weekdays.
   _____
5. Progress reports are given out once a month.
   _____

10 Practice

Read the answers. Then write information questions with the words in parentheses. Use the passive voice.

1. Q: *Why was money collected?*
   A: Money was collected for buying new trees. (*Why?*)
2. Q: _____
   A: New trees were planted in the spring. (*When?*)
3. Q: _____
   A: The festival was held in the park. (*Where?*)
4. Q: _____
   A: The festival is held every year. (*How often?*)
5. Q: _____
   A: The park is located in the center of town. (*Where?*)
6. Q: _____
   A: Everyone in the community is invited. (*Who?*)

11 Practice

Have a competition! Go to page 133.

12 Pronunciation

Sentence stress

A. **B46** Listen.

   <u>Jack</u> was <u>assigned</u> to the <u>Beach</u> <u>Cleanup</u> team.

B. **B47** Listen and repeat.
   1. The <u>beach</u> was <u>cleaned</u> last <u>weekend</u>.
   2. <u>TIG</u> was <u>set up</u> by <u>teen</u>agers.
   3. The <u>ones</u> who volun<u>teer</u>ed were <u>thanked</u>.
   4. <u>One</u> girl was <u>asked</u> to find <u>more</u> volun<u>teers</u>.

102 Unit 11

13 Vocabulary

The natural environment

A. B48 Listen and repeat.

1. cliff
2. sea/ocean
3. hill
4. lake
5. coast
6. beach
7. forest
8. mountain
9. desert

B. PAIRS. Match the words with their definitions. Write the letters.

_b_ 1. lake
___ 2. desert
___ 3. cliff
___ 4. hill
___ 5. coast
___ 6. beach
___ 7. sea/ocean
___ 8. mountain
___ 9. forest

a. sandy land near an ocean
b. water surrounded by land
c. land covered by trees
d. land that is always hot and dry
e. very high land mass
f. water that covers two-thirds of the earth
g. high land that is not as high as a mountain
h. where land and sea meet
i. very steep, high rock

TEEN TALK

Talk about the natural areas where you live and their condition.

Useful language:
- (Our coasts) are beautiful, but the tourists are ruining them.
- Have you ever been to (the lake near . . .)?
- What's it like?
- Is there any evidence of global warming in (our country)?
- I think . . . is an important environmental problem in our country.

Unit 11   103

14 Listening

B49 Listen and write *True*, *False*, or *NI* (no information).

False 1. TIG stands for Talk About It Globally.

_____ 2. Members decide how long they want to volunteer for.

_____ 3. TIG is based in Australia.

_____ 4. TIG was founded by teenagers.

_____ 5. Adults also volunteer for TIG.

15 Communication

Ask for information by telephone

A. **B50** Listen to the conversation.

A: Thank you for calling TIG. This is Pam.
B: Yes. Hello. I'm a volunteer, and I was told to call this number for information.
A: That's right. How can I help you?
B: What time are the volunteers meeting at the beach this Saturday?
A: Nine o'clock. Do you know where to go?
B: I was told to go to the Surf and Snack.
A: That's right. The team leaders will be waiting there. Is there anything else?
B: No, that's it. Thanks.

B. **PAIRS.** Role-play the telephone conversation in Exercise A, but replace the volunteer's question with a new question.

16 Your turn

GROUPS. Think about an environmental problem in your area. Think of simple ways you can help solve the problem. Present your solutions to the class.

The streets of our city are dirty. My classmates and I can go out this weekend and pick up the litter in the area near our school...

17 Writing

A. Do research on an environmental issue that you feel strongly about. Take notes. Try to include the following information in your notes:

- a description of the environmental issue
- the cause (or causes) of the problem
- a description of any organizations that are helping to solve the problem
- what we can do to help solve the problem

B. In your notebook, write two or more paragraphs about the issue based on your notes.

Learn to learn

Revise your writing.

After you've written a first draft, it's good to consider carefully what you have written and how you have expressed yourself to see how it can be improved. Always look for ways to make your writing clearer and more interesting.

A. Look at the paragraphs you wrote in Exercise 17. Use the questions below to help you make revisions to your writing.
- Are your ideas written in a logical sequence?
- Do you express your ideas with vivid, descriptive words?
- Is every word needed? Are there any unnecessary words?
- Is the spelling and punctuation correct?
- Is the grammar correct?

B. **PAIRS.** Show your classmate some of the changes you made to your writing.

Putting it together   Getting over Scott

A. B51 **Read along as you listen. What reason does Scott give for being self-centered?**

1
- Hi, Kelly. I was told I'd find you here. Can we talk?
- I'm busy, Scott. What's there to talk about, anyway?

2
- I know you're leaving soon. I'm going to miss you.
- Yeah, right!

3
- I know you think I'm a self-centered jerk. But when I was growing up, I was always told that I was the best. It's the way I was brought up.
- Uh-huh.

4
- So, I guess you came to say good-bye to Kelly.
- Yeah, and to apologize. It's not working, though.
- Try again, man. She just needs to know you really mean it.
- I'll try.

5
- Come on, Kelly. Give me another chance.
- I'll think about it.

6
- So, can I call you once in a while?
- Maybe. I have to go help Jack. Bye.

B. GROUPS. Discuss these questions: Why is Scott admitting to Kelly that he has been self-centered? Should Kelly give Scott another chance? Why or why not?

Unit 11   105

Game 4   Gossip

Steps:

1. Play this game in two teams, each team sitting in a row. Two students on each team (S1 and S2) are "talkers," while the other team members are "gossipers."

2. S1 chooses one of the tasks and makes up a question. He or she whispers the question, and S2 answers in a complete sentence. The next student in line, S3, is the only person who can hear what S1 and S2 are saying. He or she listens and quickly whispers S2's answer to the question, using *said* or *told*, to the next person in line, S4. Then S4 whispers the same information to the next person, and so on until the message reaches the last person on the team.

3. The last person on each team reports what he or she has heard, and the talkers say whether or not it is correct. Each team gets one point for a correctly reported answer.

4. S2 now chooses another task and asks S3 a question. Repeat the process until every student has had a chance to ask a question.

5. The team with the most points wins.

Tasks:

Ask a question using the simple past. ("What did you eat . . . ?")

Ask a question using the present continuous. ("What are you watching . . . ?")

Ask a question using the future with *will*. ("Will you be . . . ?")

Ask a question using the present perfect. ("Have you called . . . ?")

Ask a question using the present perfect continuous. ("What have you been studying . . . ?")

For example:

Ask a question using the past tense.

S1: Where did you go on your last date?
S2: I went to Pete's Pizza Parlor.
S3: Maria said that she had gone to Pete's Pizza Parlor on her last date.

Useful language

- Could you please repeat that?
- That's right. / That's not right.
- Our team gets a point!
- Let's try another one.

106

Project 4

A snapshot of a global issue

GROUPS. Choose a global issue that you care about. Research the issue and make a poster. Use the steps below as a guide. Display your poster so others can learn more about the issue.

1. Choose an issue from the box, or come up with your own.

   - World peace
   - Global warming
   - Endangered animals
   - Deforestation
   - Threatened coral reefs
   - Carbon emissions
   - Overpopulation
   - World poverty
   - Human rights
   - World health

DEFORESTATION

2. Research facts about the issue.

   Every minute about 149 acres (60 hectares) of the world's rain forests are destroyed to clear land for cattle farms, oil rigs, and mines. Rain forest trees are turned into paper, cardboard, and plywood.

3. Explain why it is a problem.

   Although rain forests cover only 2 percent of the earth's surface, they are home to over half of the world's plants and animals. If rain forests are destroyed, many of the world's plants and animals will die, and some species might become extinct. Native people who depend on the rain forests for their livelihood are also threatened.

4. Suggest ways for people like you to do something about the problem.

   Here are some ways that teenagers like us can help save the rain forests:
   - use less paper and gasoline
   - eat less beef
   - donate money to organizations that work to save rain forests
   - talk to friends and family about the issue
   - write letters of complaint to companies that contribute to the destruction of rain forests
   - organize a peaceful demonstration against deforestation

5. Don't forget to use drawings or photos in your posters.

Project 4   107

12 Even though he's arrogant,...

1 Dialogue

B52 Cover the dialogue and listen.

Denise: I'll miss you, Kelly. It's been great having you here.
Kelly: I loved being here. Thanks for being so understanding.
Denise: Hey, that's what friends are for. So, what did Scott say at the beach?
Kelly: He apologized, of course, and he explained why he is the way he is.
Denise: Do you think you two can still be friends?
Kelly: Maybe. Even though he's arrogant, I don't hate him. So maybe.
Jack: Hi, guys. Kelly, this is for you.
Kelly: Thanks. My favorite flower! And a poster of a surfer?
Jack: It's a great picture, isn't it? It'll remind you of your summer in California!
Kelly: There are a few things I'd rather forget!
Jack: Come on. You had fun this summer, didn't you?
Kelly: You know, in spite of Scott's behavior, I did have fun. So, see you guys next summer?
Jack: You bet. Take care.

Learning goals

Communication
Express pleasure and thanks

Grammar
Connectors: *and*, *but*, *so*, *or*
Showing contrast with *although/even though*, *in spite of*, and *however*

Vocabulary
Adjectives describing personality

108 Unit 12

2 Comprehension

A. Answer the questions.

1. What does Kelly thank Denise for being?
2. Does Kelly think she and Scott can still be friends?
3. What does Jack give Kelly? Why does he give her that gift?
4. Does Kelly plan to return to the inn next summer?

B. B53 Read along as you listen again. Check your answers.

3 Useful expressions

A. B54 Listen and repeat.

- Hey, that's what friends are for.
- You bet. Take care.
- Thanks for being so understanding.
- So, see you next summer?

B. PAIRS. Reorder the expressions in Exercise A to make a conversation. Then role-play the conversation.

A: _____
B: _____
A: _____
B: _____

4 Communication

Express pleasure and thanks

A. B55 Listen and read.

A: I really enjoyed my stay here. I had a wonderful time. Thanks for having me.
B: You're welcome. I'm glad you came.

B. PAIRS. Imagine you were invited to a party at your friend's house. Write a conversation between you and your friend's mother. You are thanking her and saying goodbye.

C. PAIRS. Practice your conversation. Then role-play it in front of another pair.

Unit 12 109

GRAMMAR FOCUS

Connectors:
and, but, so, or

Scott talked to Kelly at the beach. He apologized to her.
Scott talked to Kelly at the beach, **and** he apologized to her.

Denise wanted Kelly to stay. Kelly had to go.
Denise wanted Kelly to stay, **but** Kelly had to go.

Kelly was leaving. Jack gave her a gift.
Kelly was leaving, **so** Jack gave her a gift.

Kelly wanted Scott to apologize. If not, she would forget about him.
Kelly wanted Scott to apologize, **or** she would forget about him.

Discovering grammar

Look at the grammar chart. Complete the grammar rules using *and*, *but*, *so*, or *or*.

1. Use _____ to show an unexpected contrast.
2. Use _____ to show a consequence (usually a negative consequence).
3. Use _____ to show more information.
4. Use _____ to show a result.

Practicing grammar

5 Practice

Rewrite the following sentences using the cues. Use correct punctuation.

1. Sarah wants to be a dentist. Tom wants to be a doctor. (*but*)
   Sarah wants to be a dentist, but Tom wants to be a doctor.
2. James must study for his math test. He will not pass the test. (*or*)

3. Ed likes studying math. He is a wonderful science student. (*and*)

4. Ken likes to surf. He is not really good at surfing. (*but*)

5. Jenny was late for school. She ran all the way there. (*so*)

6. Elizabeth likes writing. She decided to keep a journal. (*so*)

6 Practice

Circle the correct connector and write it in the blanks.

1. The boy enjoyed playing golf, (*but* / **and**) __and__ his sister liked it, too.
2. The movie wasn't over, (*so* / *but*) _____ she was too sleepy to watch it to the end.
3. I have to finish my homework, (*or* / *and*) _____ I won't be allowed to play my computer game.
4. His cell phone rang, (*but* / *so*) _____ he answered it.
5. The kids were happy to be at the party, (*but* / *or*) _____ they were upset when it ended.
6. The girl is talented at soccer, (*so* / *and*) _____ she is good at tennis, too.

110 Unit 12

7 Vocabulary

Personality traits

A. **B56** Listen and repeat.

- ambitious
- arrogant
- bossy
- creative
- dependable
- good-natured
- loyal
- outgoing
- sensitive
- understanding

B. Fill in the blanks with the correct adjective.

1. A __dependable__ person can be counted on.
2. A _____ person is easygoing and doesn't get mad easily.
3. A _____ person is likely to order others around.
4. An _____ person always wants to succeed.
5. A _____ person likes to create things.
6. A _____ person is true to someone or something.
7. An _____ person thinks he or she is better than others.
8. A _____ person is easily hurt by what others do or say.
9. An _____ person shows sympathy for other people's problems.
10. An _____ person is friendly and feels comfortable in new situations.

TEEN TALK

GROUPS. Talk about what kind of people you like spending time with. Decide what personality traits you like or dislike in a person.

Useful language:
- I like people who are . . .
- I like my friends to be . . .
- If I were choosing a leader, he or she would have to be . . .
- I don't like being with people who are . . .
- I know what you mean.
- Yeah, I know people like that.

8 Your turn

A. Write an example of a behavior that demonstrates each trait.

1. outgoing _This person feels comfortable at a party, even when he or she doesn't know anyone._
2. dependable _____
3. good-natured _____
4. kind _____
5. creative _____
6. understanding _____

B. PAIRS. Read one of your sentences in Exercise A to your classmate. See if your classmate can identify which trait it's describing. Take turns.

C. Think of three adjectives that describe your personality. Use your dictionary if you need to. Write the adjectives in the boxes.

D. GROUPS. Have one person in your group collect your books. He or she reads the personality traits written in Exercise C. The others guess who the book belongs to.

Unit 12 111

GRAMMAR FOCUS

Showing contrast with *although/even though*, *in spite of*, **and** *however*

Even though he's arrogant, she likes him.
Although he's arrogant, she likes him.
In spite of Scott's behavior, Kelly enjoyed herself.

She likes him **even though** he's arrogant.
She likes him **although** he's arrogant.
Kelly enjoyed herself **in spite of** Scott's behavior.

He's arrogant. **However**, Kelly still likes him.

Discovering grammar

Look at the grammar chart. Circle the correct answers.

1. Sentences that start with *although* or *even though* need (*one* / *two*) clauses.
2. Sentences that start with *in spite of* need (*one* / *two*) clauses.
3. *In spite of* (*can* / *can't*) be followed by a noun phrase.
4. When you make a contrast, you (*can* / *can't*) start a sentence with *however*.

Practicing grammar

9 Practice

Complete the sentences with *even though* (or *although*), *however*, **or** *in spite of*.

1. *Even though* Janet doesn't need a new watch, she still bought one.
2. _____ Bill learned Chinese, he had no plans to travel to China.
3. My sneakers are old. _____, I still use them.
4. I feel hungry _____ the big breakfast I ate this morning.
5. My sister really likes these CDs _____ she never listens to them.
6. _____ she misses her family, she likes being in college.
7. My baby brother annoys me. _____, I still love him.
8. _____ we're classmates, we don't see each other very much.
9. Jane was 12 years old. _____, she still needed a sitter when her parents went out.
10. We went for a walk _____ the cold weather.

10 Practice

Rewrite the following sentences. Replace *even though* **with** *in spite of*.

1. Jenny slept well even though the party was noisy.
   Jenny slept well in spite of the noisy party.
2. The park was full of people even though the weather was bad.
   _____
   _____
3. She didn't reach the finals even though her performance in the semifinals was amazing.
   _____
   _____
4. He enjoyed the evening even though he had a terrible cold.
   _____
   _____

112 Unit 12

11 Practice

Write your own sentences using the cues in parentheses. Add commas where needed.

1. It's still hot in here . . . (*even though*)
   It's still hot in here even though we opened the windows.

2. . . . we rarely see each other. (*although*)
   Although we're neighbors, we rarely see each other.

3. John competed in the race . . . (*in spite of*)

4. Dad wasn't feeling well. (*however*)

5. They walked home . . . (*in spite of*)

6. I fed my dog twice. (*however*)

7. . . . I had a cold. (*although*)

12 Practice

Have a competition! Go to page 133.

13 Pronunciation

Use intonation to show contrast

A. **B57** Listen.

Scott was showing off, but his friend seemed nice.
Even though I wanted to leave, I stayed a few more minutes.
I didn't study. However, I think I'll do OK on the quiz.

B. **B58** Listen and repeat. Try to imitate the intonation pattern you hear.

1. Although Jamie tried to be careful, he still fell on the ice.
2. In spite of the mess in her bedroom, Cassidy found her wallet.
3. Ken liked his presents. However, what he really wanted was a new bicycle.
4. White sneakers are OK, but I like black sneakers better.
5. Even though Jason is my best friend, I like to hang out with Alex, too.

14 Listening

B59 Melinda spent a month on a homestay visit in Spain. When she returned home, she sent her host family a video clip. Read these questions. Then listen for the answers.

1. Where is Melinda standing in her video clip?
2. When was she in Spain?
3. How good is her Spanish?
4. How was the weather in Spain during her visit?
5. Where does Melinda live in the United States?
6. What does she want her host family to do next summer?
7. What would she like them to bring?

Unit 12 113

15 Reading

B60 Read along silently as you listen. What kind of friendship did Helen and Anne have?

Friends for Life

When Helen Keller was two years old, a fever left her blind and deaf. Frustrated and confused, Helen struggled to cope with her condition, and she became a difficult child to manage. "Even though I moved my lips, nothing happened," she later wrote. "This made me angry, so I would kick and scream until I was exhausted."

Then in March 1887, Helen's life took an unexpected turn for the better. Anne Sullivan accepted a job as Helen's governess. She began to teach the frustrated young girl to communicate. She started by spelling out words on her hand. One day, they went to the water pump outside the house. As the water flowed over one of Helen's hands, Anne spelled the word *w-a-t-e-r* on the other hand. Suddenly, the letters meant something to the little girl. Helen touched the pump and asked its name. By nightfall, Helen had learned thirty words. It was a most exciting day!

Although she could neither see nor hear, Helen's ability to learn was phenomenal. In spite of her enormous handicap, she graduated with honors from Radcliffe College. Throughout her college years, Anne was by her side, spelling out book after book, lecture after lecture, on her pupil's hand. When Helen became famous, Anne continued to travel with her, interpreting sentence by sentence both for Helen and for her audiences.

Helen led a most remarkable life. She traveled all over the world fighting for civil and women's rights, human dignity, and world peace. She was always searching for ways to help the blind, the less fortunate, and those "who struggled for justice." Until Anne's death in 1936, she supported Helen in everything she did, as an interpreter, as a teacher, and as a friend.

16 Comprehension

Answer the questions.

1. Why was Helen always angry as a child?
2. How did Anne teach Helen the meanings of words?
3. How did Helen manage to go to college and get a degree?
4. What world issues did Helen fight for as an adult?

17 Speaking

GROUPS. Discuss these questions.

1. How did Anne's friendship help Helen achieve her goals?
2. What makes Helen an extraordinary person?

> **Learn to learn**
>
> **Find the main idea: topic sentences.**
>
> Identifying the main idea of a paragraph is a useful reading skill. It prepares you for what you will be reading about. Often the main idea is stated directly and can be found in a topic sentence. The other sentences in the paragraph support and develop the main idea.
>
> Look at the reading in Exercise 15 and underline the topic sentences (in this case, they are the first sentences in each paragraph). Notice how the other sentences in each paragraph develop the main idea.

18 Writing

A. Write two or three paragraphs in your notebook about someone who has had a positive influence on you. It might be someone you know personally or someone you read or learned about. Explain how this person has influenced you. Be sure to include a topic sentence in each of your paragraphs.

B. **PAIRS.** Read and comment on your classmate's writing. Use the Peer editing checklist on page 134 to help you.

Progress check — Units 11 and 12

Test-taking tip: Learn from your tests.
Make sure you understand your mistakes. If you got a wrong answer and you don't know what the answer should have been, look it up, or ask a classmate or the teacher.

Grammar

A. Change the following active sentences into passive sentences. In your notebook, write the new sentences, using *by* + person where appropriate. (3 points each)

1. Rudyard Kipling wrote *The Jungle Book*.
   The Jungle Book was written by Rudyard Kipling.
2. Picasso painted *Guernica*.
3. Many people in Singapore speak Chinese.
4. They built the tomb of Tutankhamun in the Valley of the Kings.
5. Marie Curie discovered radium in 1898.
6. Walt Disney created Disneyland as a playground for his daughter.

B. In your notebook, write information questions about the sentences in Exercise A. Use the passive voice and the cues. (3 points each)

1. (What book)
   What book was written by Rudyard Kipling?
2. (What)
3. (What language)
4. (Where)
5. (When)
6. (Why)

C. Complete the sentences. Use words from the box. (2 points each)

| ~~although~~ | however | or |
| and | in spite of | so |

1. _Although_ I'm scared of sharks, I like swimming in the ocean.
2. We have to take care of our coral reefs, _____ in the future there will be none left.
3. There's a drought in our city, _____ we're not allowed to wash our cars.
4. My grandparents like living in the desert _____ the hot climate.
5. The rainforests are being destroyed. _____, it's not too late to save them.
6. Global warming is a big problem, _____ it's getting worse.

Vocabulary

D. Match the sentences to the adjectives. Write the letter in the blanks. (1 point each)

a. bossy   c. dependable   e. shy
b. competitive   d. easygoing

_d_ 1. I don't get upset easily. I'm . . .
___ 2. I'm always there to help. I'm . . .
___ 3. I don't want to be on stage. I'm too . . .
___ 4. I love it when I win. I'm . . .
___ 5. I like to tell people what do do. I'm . . .

Communication

E. Imagine you spent your summer vacation with a family friend, and you had a wonderful time. In your notebook, write a conversation with your friend, expressing thanks and pleasure. (5 points)

Now I can . . .
❏ get information by telephone.
❏ express pleasure and thanks.
❏ show contrast.

Wide Angle on the world

1 Reading

> **Reading skill:** Separating fact from opinion
> When you read, try to identify which statements are facts and which are opinions. This can help you decide if an article is useful or not.

A. Read the article. Underline two facts. Circle details that support the facts. Draw a box around statements that give opinions. Underline words that show it's an opinion.

B. Read the article again. Then answer the questions.

1. How are a greenhouse and the atmosphere alike?
   _____

2. What happens when polar ice caps and glaciers melt?
   _____

3. Why are people worried about global warming?
   _____

4. What is a major cause of pollution?
   _____

2 Listening

B61 Listen to the presentation. Circle the answers.

1. The blue team's idea was to:
   a. ask people to drive less.
   b. encourage people to keep their tires well inflated.
2. According to the presentation, for every gallon of gas we use,
   a. 20 pounds of carbon dioxide goes into the atmosphere.
   b. 30 pounds of carbon dioxide goes into the atmosphere.
3. The students wanted people to be aware of
   a. the effects of low tire pressure.
   b. how they could save money on gas.

3 Speaking

GROUPS. Discuss these questions:

Should we worry about global warming? Should world governments do more about this issue?

4 Writing

Write a short summary of your group's opinions based on your notes. Then share the summary with the class.

116 Wide Angle 4

It's Getting Hot in Here

Have you ever been to a greenhouse? Greenhouses are made of glass. The glass traps heat from the sun so the plants inside can grow even when it's very cold outside. Earth's atmosphere is like a greenhouse. The atmosphere is a layer of gases that traps enough heat from the sun so that humans and other living things can survive. But there is a problem. Pollution has started to enter the atmosphere. More pollution in the atmosphere means more heat is trapped. Scientists say this is causing Earth's climate to gradually become warmer. In fact, a study shows that the past decade was the hottest of the past 150 years, perhaps longer.

So, it's getting warmer outside. Some people think a few degrees isn't important, and there is nothing to worry about. But even very small changes in the Earth's climate can have a big impact. When the Earth's climate gets hotter, polar ice caps and glaciers melt. This causes the ocean levels to rise. A study shows that the flow of ice from Greenland has more than doubled over the last decade. Some people say global warming might change the environment so much that plants, animals, and even humans will be in danger.

Pollution from automobiles is a big part of the problem. What can we do? Many people say it's impossible to stop using gasoline altogether. Other people think we should find alternative fuels and use our energy more efficiently.

What can you do to make a difference? Here are some easy ways that you can help save energy and fight global warming:

- Walk, ride a bike, or use public transportation instead of going places by car.
- Conserve energy! When you are not using appliances, turn them off. Turn off lights, TVs, and computers when you leave a room.
- Recycle whenever you can. Recycling helps to save energy.

Fun with songs 1

A list of our favorite songs

A. **GROUPS.** On a piece of paper, make two columns with the heads *Favorite English songs* and *Favorite local songs*.

B. **GROUPS.** Talk about your favorite songs. Choose two or three songs for each column. List their titles and the names of the singers. Use the Useful language in your discussion.

C. **GROUPS.** Present your list to the class. Write the song titles and the singers' names on the board.

D. **CLASS.** Look at the titles on the board. Vote for your top three favorite songs in each category. Copy the titles of the top songs into your notebook.

E. *Homework*: Listen to as many of the songs on the class list as you can. Which songs do you like best? Why?

F. **CLASS.** Share your reactions to the songs with your classmates.

Useful language:
- What's your favorite song?
- Same here. / Not me.
- Yeah, that's a great song.
- I haven't heard of him/her/them.
- What kind of music do they play?
- I'm into love songs.
- Really? What do you like about them?
- That song's too romantic.

Fun with songs 2

A booklet of favorite songs

THE BEST OF THE BEST

Materials:
- Lyrics to favorite songs
- Pictures to illustrate the booklet
- Markers or colored pencils
- Paper for each group's booklet

A. **GROUPS.** Look at the list of songs you made in Fun with songs 1. Each group member should choose one favorite song from the list.

B. *Homework*: Each group member should look for:
- the lyrics to the song
- biographical information about the singer or group
- pictures to illustrate the song and booklet

C. **GROUPS.** Put your booklet together. Use the Useful language in your discussion. Discuss:
- how to organize the songs and biographies
- the title for the collection
- the decorations for the pages and the cover

D. **GROUPS.** Present your song book to the class. If there's time, play one song from the collection and share some information about the singer or group. Ask your classmates for their comments and questions.

E. **CLASS.** Vote on the following:
- The best presentation
- The most creative song collection
- Your favorite song collection

Useful language:
- If I had to choose my top favorite song, I guess it would be . . .
- It'd be good to include . . .
- How should we organize the songs?
- How about by genre or alphabetically according to the titles?
- That's a really good idea.
- We need to decide or we won't be able to finish this on time.

Fun with songs 3

A rebus of a favorite song

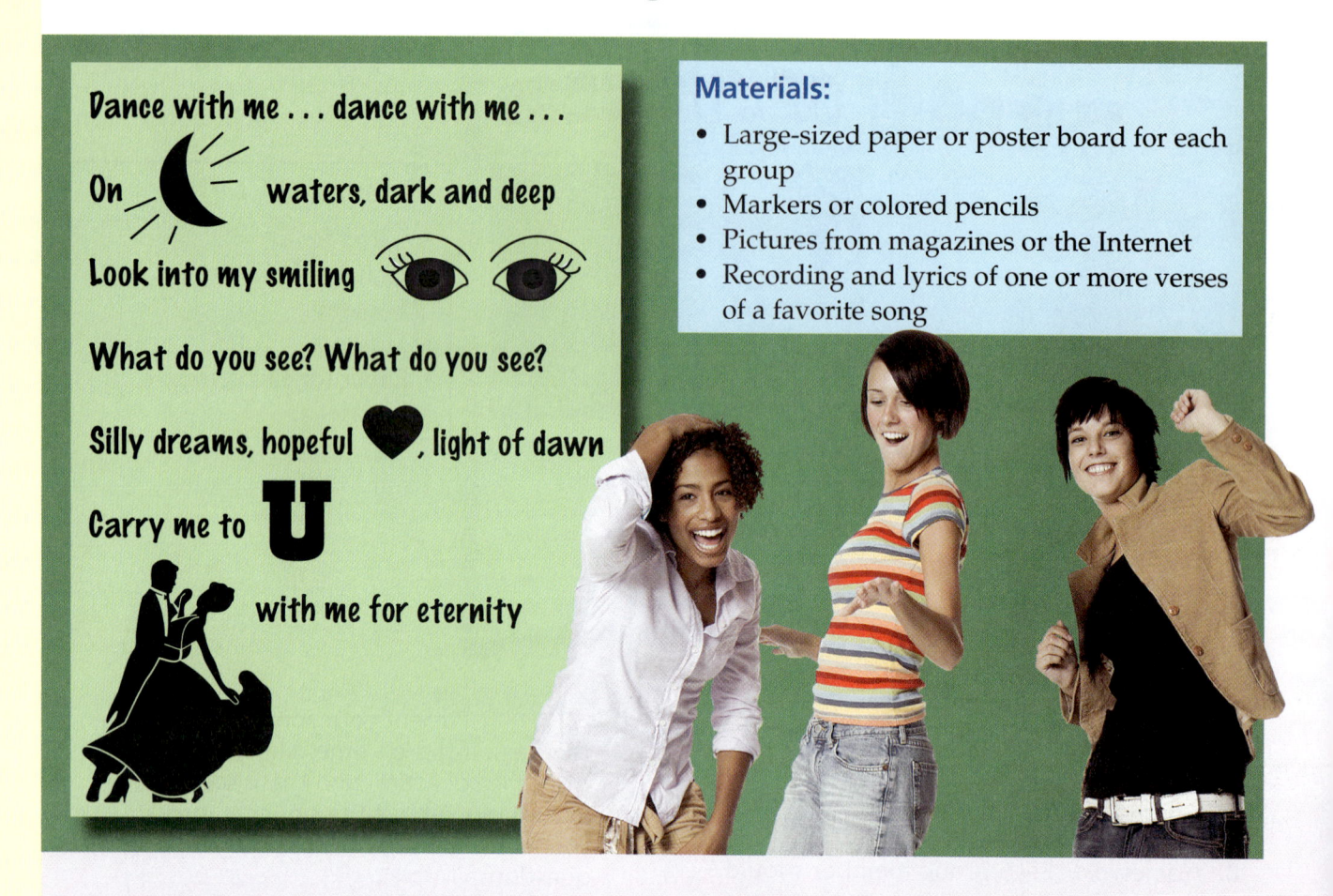

Dance with me... dance with me...

On 🌙 waters, dark and deep

Look into my smiling 👀

What do you see? What do you see?

Silly dreams, hopeful ♥, light of dawn

Carry me to U

💃 with me for eternity

Materials:
- Large-sized paper or poster board for each group
- Markers or colored pencils
- Pictures from magazines or the Internet
- Recording and lyrics of one or more verses of a favorite song

A. **GROUPS.** Choose a favorite song. Choose one person in your group to bring a recording of the song to class.

B. *Homework*: Find the lyrics of the song you chose in Step A. Find pictures that illustrate some of the words in the lyrics. Bring your pictures to class.

C. **GROUPS.** Discuss the song. Use some of the Useful language in your discussion. Create a rebus for the song. Choose someone to write the lyrics on a large piece of paper or poster board. Discuss which words you want to replace with pictures. Either draw pictures you need for your rebus or use pictures that you've found in magazines or on the Internet. Glue your pictures in place.

D. **GROUPS.** Exchange your rebus with another group. Figure out what words the pictures or drawings represent. Sing the song (or read it aloud) to the class using the rebus. Then listen to the recording of the song to see how you did.

Useful language:
- I think we should . . .
- I think so, too.
- That might work.
- Go ahead and try that.
- I'm not sure I agree with you.
- I'll put this here.
- That's a perfect picture for that word!
- What word is that supposed to be a picture of?

Fun with songs 4

A favorite song in mime

> Boys call me day and night
> And they're all right,
> Yes, they're all right;
> But I say no, it's just not me,
> I'm waiting for you,
> Waiting for you,
> Waiting for my one and only you.

Materials:
- Copies of the lyrics of a favorite song, cut up into separate lines
- Recording of the song

A. CLASS. Form teams. Your teacher will give your team several lines from a favorite song. Your task is to mime the lines to the class.

B. GROUPS. Read the song lines that your teacher gives you. Discuss their meaning. Use a dictionary if helpful. Discuss how to mime the lines. Then practice miming them. Remember that you can't use any words while you're miming your lines.

C. GROUPS. Each group will present their mime in the order that the lines appear in the song. The lines from the song will be played while each team mimes the lines.

D. CLASS. Discuss the presentation. Did it work? Did the groups understand each other's mimes? Would you do it differently next time? Classmates can give miming ideas for other groups' mimes.

Useful language:
- Do you have any ideas?
- Maybe we should do it like this. Look.
- We'd better hurry and think of something.
- This line is hard to mime, isn't it?
- What did you think of our idea?
- I think your group should have . . .

Focus on culture 1

A Day in the Life of a Japanese Teenager

It's Friday morning in Tokyo. Seventeen-year-old Akiko gets up at 6:30 as usual. She takes a quick shower and gets dressed in the dark blue-and-white school uniform that most Japanese students wear. Then she eats salad, vegetables, fish, and rice for breakfast, grabs her lunch box, and heads for the train station.

During the commute, she checks her cell phone to see if she has any e-mail messages. Like most teenagers in Japan, Akiko uses her cell phone to talk to her friends, send and receive e-mail, surf the Internet, take pictures, and film videos. Akiko has ten messages this morning, including this short message from her boyfriend, Kazu: "Good morning!" It's 8:20 when Akiko arrives at school. Her classes begin at 8:30 and end at 3:30.

After school, Akiko goes to her English and calligraphy club meetings. Then Akiko goes to a private cram school called a "juku." The juku helps her to prepare for the difficult entrance exams she must pass in order to get into one of the top government-run universities. She studies at the juku for an hour and a half after school each day during the week, and six hours on Saturdays.

Akiko gets home at 7:30. She eats dinner with her family, does about an hour and a half of homework, and then soaks in the family's deep bathtub. After checking her e-mail again, she goes to her bedroom and quickly falls asleep.

Sunday is Akiko's free day. She often takes the train into Harajuku, a trendy shopping district for teenagers in central Tokyo, to meet Kazu. His hair is dyed the fashionable reddish brown color that many Japanese teenagers favor. He likes to mix California surfer wear with the latest Japanese and British fashions.

Akiko and Kazu look at clothes. Then they head over to Yoyogi Park to listen to some of the bands playing. Akiko has to be home by 6:30, so Kazu walks her back to the station and says good-bye. On the train, Akiko checks her e-mail one last time. There's a message from Kazu: "I had fun with you today." Akiko smiles and quickly types her response: "Me, too!"

1 Comprehension

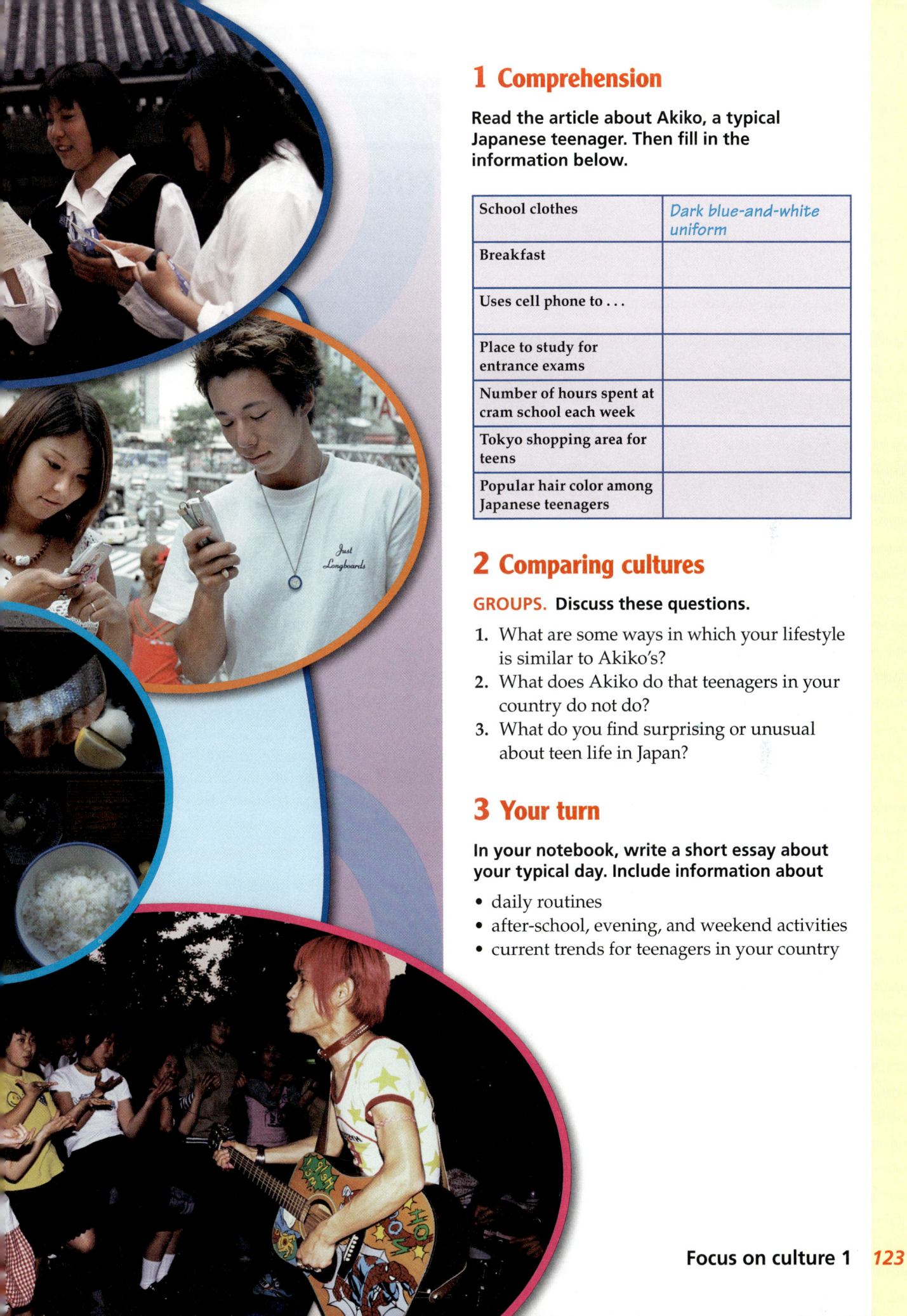

Read the article about Akiko, a typical Japanese teenager. Then fill in the information below.

School clothes	Dark blue-and-white uniform
Breakfast	
Uses cell phone to . . .	
Place to study for entrance exams	
Number of hours spent at cram school each week	
Tokyo shopping area for teens	
Popular hair color among Japanese teenagers	

2 Comparing cultures

GROUPS. Discuss these questions.

1. What are some ways in which your lifestyle is similar to Akiko's?
2. What does Akiko do that teenagers in your country do not do?
3. What do you find surprising or unusual about teen life in Japan?

3 Your turn

In your notebook, write a short essay about your typical day. Include information about

- daily routines
- after-school, evening, and weekend activities
- current trends for teenagers in your country

Focus on culture 1   123

Focus on culture 2

Visiting Homes across Cultures

Frequent air travel and the Internet have enabled many of us to make friends from other cultures. Sometimes, these friends invite us to visit them in their native countries. If you are invited to a foreign friend's home, it is important to familiarize yourself with the local customs. If you keep these local "rules" in mind, you won't make any embarrassing mistakes, and you'll have a very warm and pleasant visit.

Koreans and Japanese know how to make guests feel special, though the atmosphere in their homes can seem quite formal to people from some other cultures. When visiting the home of a Korean or Japanese family, it is considered polite to bring a gift. Common gifts are food, flowers, or a souvenir from your country. But never give a gift of four items, since the number four signifies death in these cultures. Be sure to give and receive gifts with both hands to show respect. If the gift is wrapped, your host will open it after you leave. When sitting, it is polite to keep your feet on the floor. You shouldn't stretch out your legs. You shouldn't be too talkative at mealtimes; instead, quietly appreciate the food.

When you visit a Middle Eastern home, your host will usually take you into a special room for guests. When you enter, everyone will stand up. It is important that you greet each person individually, starting with the person on your right. When shaking hands, always use your right hand, as the left hand is considered dirty. You should also use only your right hand to take food or drink. It is not necessary to bring a gift, but chocolate or baked goods will be appreciated. Don't hand a gift directly to your host, but instead quietly put your gift in the room just before you leave. Your host will find it and will open it after you leave.

Meanwhile, a typical North American family will most likely greet you at the door with a casual "Hi. How are you?" It is not common to bring a gift unless you'll be staying for a few days. If you do bring a gift, you should give it directly to your hosts, who will unwrap it immediately and say how much they like it. North Americans are quite proud of their houses, so it is fine to ask for a tour of the house and to compliment things you like. After a meal, remember that it is always polite to offer to help clean up. But the most important rule to remember is that your hosts will usually be happiest if you are relaxed and casual.

1 Comprehension

Where are the following customs practiced? Write *KJ* for Korea and Japan, *ME* for the Middle East, and *NA* for North America.

_ME_ 1. When you arrive, greet everyone, beginning on your right.

____ 2. Always bring a gift when visiting someone's home.

____ 3. Don't give four of anything as a gift.

____ 4. Expect your host to unwrap your gift in front of you.

____ 5. Don't hand a gift directly to your host.

____ 6. Ask for a tour of the house.

____ 7. Be fairly quiet while eating.

____ 8. Never use your left hand to shake hands or take food or drink.

____ 9. Offer to help clean up after a meal.

2 Comparing cultures

GROUPS. Discuss these questions.

1. What are the do's and don'ts to keep in mind when visiting homes in the following regions?
   a. Korea and Japan
   b. the Middle East
   c. North America
2. Which customs mentioned in the article are different from the customs in your country? Which customs are similar?
3. What other do's and don'ts should foreigners keep in mind when visiting homes in your country?

3 Your turn

GROUPS. Make a poster about the do's and don'ts that people should keep in mind when visiting someone's home in your country. Include customs such as:

- how to greet people in a host's home
- gift giving
- dining etiquette

Focus on culture 3

What Is a Friend?

Omkar, 15, India

Relationships: I try not to be too selfish. I think about the needs of others.
Money: If a friend needs money, I'll lend it to him or her. If I need money, I know my friends will lend it to me.
Problems: If a friend has a problem, he or she can call anytime. I'll be there to help.
Expressing opinions: I can't be too honest with my opinions. If I say something negative, I might hurt someone's feelings.

Sara, 17, United States

Relationships: I think friends should help each other, but I don't let people take advantage of me.
Money: It's not a good idea to lend friends money. If they didn't pay me back, I'd be angry.
Problems: I don't like it when friends are too needy. People should be independent and take care of their own problems.
Expressing opinions: People shouldn't lie. It's better to be honest with one's opinions.

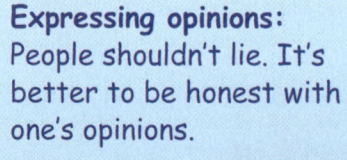

WE and ME Cultures

Ideas about friendship differ from culture to culture. Some social psychologists claim that cultures can be divided into "we" cultures and "me" cultures.

People in "we" cultures see themselves first and foremost as members of a group—a family, a school, a neighborhood, or a community. They put the needs of the group over their own needs. They know that the group, in turn, will take care of their needs. People in this type of culture know they can borrow from others when they need to. People in "we" cultures usually try not to say or do anything that will hurt a member of the group. Friendships are usually very close and last a long time. But it may be harder to make new friends in "we" cultures because people are more selective about whom they choose to open up to.

In "me" cultures, on the other hand, a person's needs, goals, and happiness are very important. People in this type of culture try to be independent and self-reliant. They strive to give their opinions honestly and directly, even if these opinions are hurtful to others. They feel that it is rude to demand too much of their friends' time, help, or money. According to some researchers, making friends in "me" cultures is very easy, but these friendships may be more superficial than in "we" cultures. Though people may have many friends, their friendships may not last as long or be as close as in "we" cultures.

When someone from a "we" culture makes friends with someone from a "me" culture, it is important that each person try to understand the other's culture. Intercultural friendships can be some of the richest and most rewarding relationships a person can have. They can open a person's eyes to a different way of viewing the world and the people in it.

1 Comprehension

A. Reread what Omkar and Sara have to say about friendship. Whose views do you agree with more? Check (✔) your answer.

_____ Omkar

_____ Sara

B. Write W for "we" cultures or M for "me" cultures next to each statement below.

_M_ 1. Friendships can be superficial.

_____ 2. You should always be honest when giving an opinion.

_____ 3. You should think about other people's needs, not only your own.

_____ 4. It's fine to borrow money from friends.

_____ 5. Your friends are there to help you.

2 Comparing cultures

Groups. Discuss these questions.

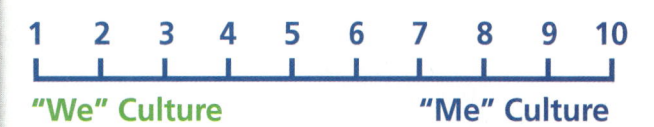

```
1   2   3   4   5   6   7   8   9   10
|   |   |   |   |   |   |   |   |   |
"We" Culture              "Me" Culture
```

1. Where would you place your culture on the scale? Circle the number. Where would you place your own personality? Draw a box around the number.
2. What do you like about "we" cultures? What don't you like?
3. What do you like about "me" cultures? What don't you like?

3 Your turn

In your notebook, write about your views of what it means to be a friend. Use Omkar's and Sara's opinions on friendship as models.

Focus on culture 3

Focus on culture 4

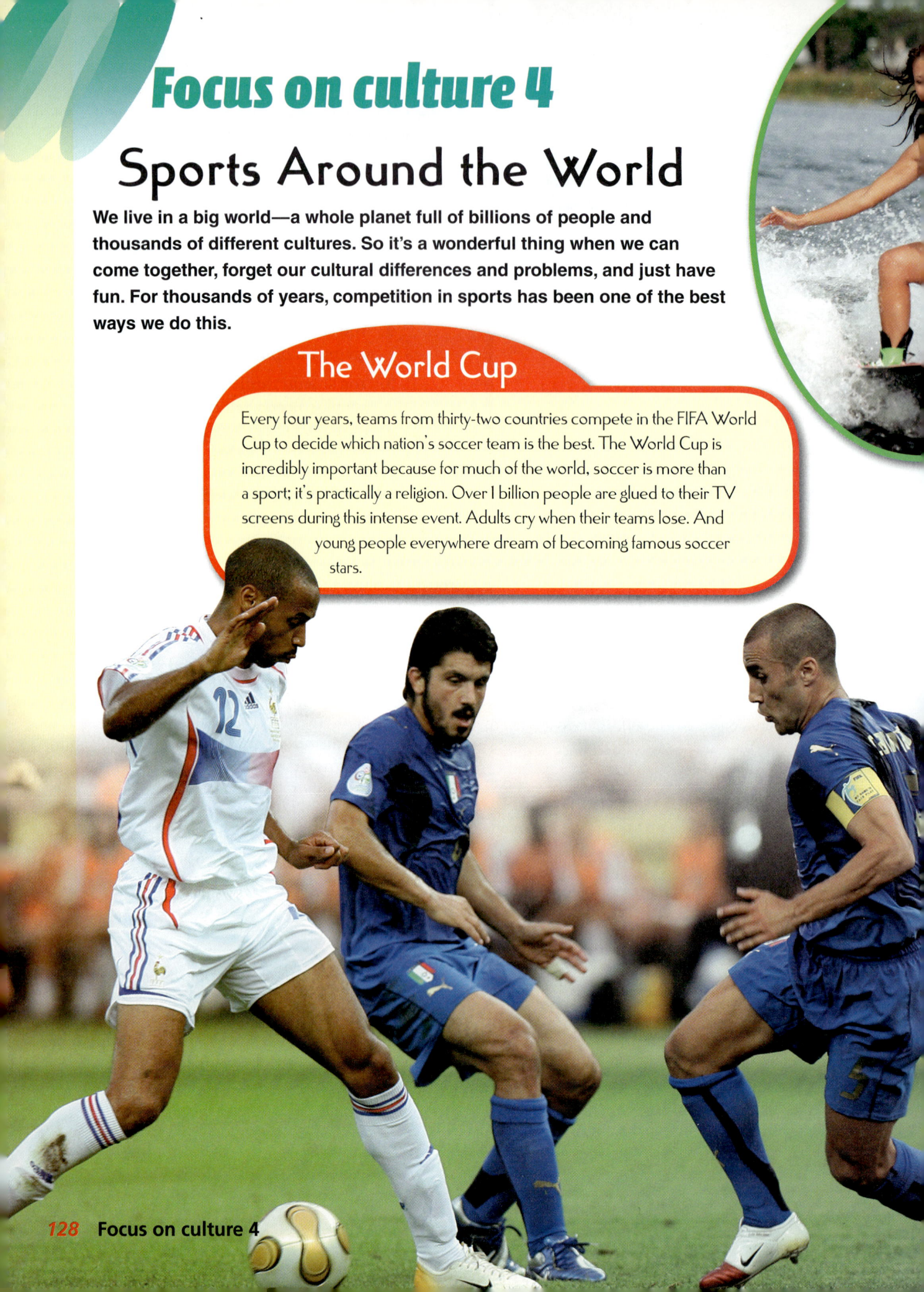

Sports Around the World

We live in a big world—a whole planet full of billions of people and thousands of different cultures. So it's a wonderful thing when we can come together, forget our cultural differences and problems, and just have fun. For thousands of years, competition in sports has been one of the best ways we do this.

The World Cup

Every four years, teams from thirty-two countries compete in the FIFA World Cup to decide which nation's soccer team is the best. The World Cup is incredibly important because for much of the world, soccer is more than a sport; it's practically a religion. Over 1 billion people are glued to their TV screens during this intense event. Adults cry when their teams lose. And young people everywhere dream of becoming famous soccer stars.

The X Games

Extreme speed, extreme height, danger, or spectacular stunts put the "X" in the X Games, which began in 1996. Each year the best extreme athletes compete in this international competition. Young athletes rule. They push themselves to the limits of their physical and mental abilities in events like BMX freestyle, wakeboarding, and motocross. Because of its popularity, X Games sports quickly give rise to new, hip trends in clothing, fashion, and music.

The Olympic Games

The first Olympic Games were held in Greece in 776 B.C. For one day every four years, all wars stopped and the best athletes from the Greek city-states had the chance to gain a lifetime of honor and glory. Gradually, the number of days increased to five. People put aside their everyday tasks and turned their attention toward the Games and the athletes who were competing in them. There were foot races and horse races; there was wrestling and discus-throwing; the air was filled with music and singing. People came together as a community. Today, the Games are still charged with the spirit of honest competition, fun times, and music. But now every two years, we celebrate either the Summer or the Winter Olympic Games. Lasting for several weeks, the Games take place in a different city each time, and top-level athletes from the world over compete in such modern events as baseball, tae-kwon-do, track and field, figure skating, and even extreme snowboarding.

1 Comprehension

Decide which statements are about the international sporting events discussed in the reading. Write *OG* for Olympic Games, *XG* for *X* Games, and *WC* for World Cup.

_WC_ 1. It focuses on a single sport.
_____ 2. It is the oldest.
_____ 3. It creates trends for teens.
_____ 4. It has a competition for track and field.
_____ 5. It is only for new and dangerous sports.
_____ 6. It began in 1996.
_____ 7. It involves roughly 32 countries.
_____ 8. It takes place every year.

2 Comparing cultures

GROUPS. Discuss these questions.

1. Why do you think international sporting events are important?
2. What is the most popular sport in your country? Does it have a positive or negative effect on people?

3 Your Turn

If you could compete in the Olympic Games, the X Games, or the World Cup, which would you choose? Why? Write about it in your notebook.

Focus on culture 4

Fun with grammar

Unit 1, 4 Practice, page 7

For the teacher: Write the following verb phrases on individual slips of paper and put them in a box.

do the tango	do the laundry
take your dog for a walk	apologize to someone
play a video game	come in late to class
ride a motorcycle	have a scary dream
eat a spicy meal	try to cross a busy street
read a cartoon	change a baby's diaper

Divide the class into two teams. Call on a student from one team and have him or her take a slip of paper from the box. This student reads silently what's written on the paper and acts it out. It's OK for the student to speak or add sound effects while acting, but he or she shouldn't speak directly to the class. The team has to guess what their classmate is doing. If the team guesses the action correctly in 30 seconds, it gets a point. Only answers using the present continuous get points.

Unit 3, 10 Practice, page 27

For the teacher: Copy the following questions onto pieces of paper. (Add more questions, if you wish.) Make enough copies to distribute to your students.

_____ 1. You don't like meat, _____?
_____ 2. You don't watch TV a lot, _____?
_____ 3. You love homework, _____?
_____ 4. You're a fan of hip-hop music, _____?
_____ 5. You go to bed before eleven, _____?
_____ 6. You aren't into sports, _____?

Tell the class to write the tag questions as quickly as they can. Give them one or two minutes to complete the activity. They may work in pairs or individually. At your signal, everyone puts his or her pen down. Correct the answers as a class. Next, have students circulate and ask their classmates the questions. Write the following on the board as a model for the answers: *You're right. I don't like meat.* OR *You're wrong. I like meat.* When a classmate answers *You're right, I . . .* , the student writes down that person's name in the blank on the left and moves on to the next question. The first student to fill in the blanks with names for all the questions wins.

Unit 2, 12 Practice, page 18

For the student: Look at the list of phrases. With a classmate, take turns making questions using the phrases. You don't have to answer the questions yet. Do this quickly. For example: (be in a snowstorm) *Have you ever been in a snowstorm?*

- be in a snowstorm
- see a magic show
- paint your bedroom by yourself
- write an article for a magazine or newspaper
- ride an elephant
- build a toy boat out of paper
- make breakfast for your parents

Divide into groups and stand in a row. S1 at the front of the row asks S2 one of the questions. S2 answers, "Yes, I have" or "No, I haven't." S2 turns around and asks S3 the same question. The game continues until the end of the row is reached. Then reverse directions. This time, the person in the back asks a question that the next person must answer, and that person then asks the next person, and so on. Do the activity quickly. The first team to go up and down the row four times is the winner.

Unit 4, 8 Practice, page 36

For the teacher: Act out an activity for the class (for example, ride my bicycle). It's important to act as though you've been riding all day, so you seem very tired. Ask the class, "What have I been doing all day?" Elicit the answer "You've been riding your bicycle all day." Divide the class into two teams. Ask a volunteer from Team 1 to act out an activity. Whisper an activity to him or her. That student acts out the activity, and his or her team gets the first chance to guess. Be sure students use the present perfect continuous. If the team is unable to guess, they pass, and the other team gets the chance to steal the point. Once all activities have been acted out, add up each team's points. The team that guessed the most activities wins.

Suggested activities (some of them can be silly, if you want):

dance	make cookies	shop
do homework	read my book	talk on the phone
juggle	ride my bicycle	write in my journal

Unit 5, 6 Practice, page 44

For the teacher: Photocopy the chart and distribute it to the class. Tell the class to complete the chart as fast as they can. Give them two minutes. Then correct the answers as a class.

Adverb	Comparative form	Superlative form
1. fast	faster	the fastest
2. badly		
3. hard		
4. slowly		
5. well		
6. successfully		
7. late		
8. carefully		
9. far		

Put students in pairs. Have them make up a sentence using one of the forms in the chart. Students should try to make the sentences as interesting as possible. Put examples on the board. *For example:*

> My mom drives fast, but my grandma drives faster.
>
> Can . . . you . . . speak . . . more . . . slowly . . . than . . . this?

Students read their sentences aloud. The class chooses their top three favorite sentences.

Unit 6, 12 Practice, page 56

For the teacher: Divide the class into pairs. Write phrases on the board. You may use the following sentences or make up your own.

- leave the party soon
- go to the mall this weekend
- use that blue marker for your poster
- call Mark sometime this weekend

Write the following model on the board and have two volunteers read it aloud:

S1: Will you be leaving the party soon?
S2: Yes, I will.
S1: Can you give me a ride home?
S2: Sure. No problem.

Have pairs work together to write a conversation based on one of the phrases on the board. Specify that their opening line must use the future continuous. The completed conversations can be funny or serious. Have pairs memorize their conversations and role-play them in front of the class. The class votes on their favorite conversation (the funniest or most clever one).

Fun with grammar   131

Unit 7, 9 Practice, page 65

For the teacher: Bring a group of six students to the front of the class to model the activity. Give each student one of the clauses below on a strip of paper. Tell students they must quickly memorize their clause.

- If I lived near a lake,
- I'd own a boat.
- If I owned a boat,
- I'd have to clean it all the time.
- If I had to clean my boat all the time,
- I'd get tired of it and I'd sell it.

Scramble the students and have each one say his or her clause aloud. The rest of the class listens. Then they direct the six students to stand in a different order and say their clauses aloud again. The goal is for the three full sentences to be said aloud in a logical order. Create other sentences similar to the model. Distribute them to the other groups of six students and have them repeat the activity.

Unit 8, 12 Practice, page 75

For the teacher: Explain to the class that they will be given the beginning of a story. Their job is to complete the story using the past perfect tense as much as possible.

Model the following story: *I never had a pet until I got a dog as a present. I had always wanted one but my parents had refused. So when the doorbell rang and I opened it, I couldn't believe my eyes . . .*

Prepare story opener sentences and put them in a box. Divide the class into groups of three or four. Have a representative from each group draw a piece of paper from the box. Each group then writes a short story using the beginning sentence they have picked. Remind them to use the past perfect tense whenever they can. Invite volunteers to read their finished stories to the class.

Suggested story openers:
- Samuel really wanted to talk to Claudia. He had already left her three messages.
- I met a new student yesterday. But I had seen him somewhere before.
- By the time I arrived at the auditorium, the concert had already started.

Unit 9, 7 Practice, page 83

For the teacher: Divide the class into two teams (Teams A and B). Give each team it's own list of sentences with quoted speech. Use a variety of tenses. *For example:*

1. Darla said, "I love doing homework on the weekend."
2. Mark said, "I'm having a lot of fun."
3. Stephanie said, "I studied until 11:30 P.M."
4. Ana said, "I can study while listening to music."
5. Julio said, "I've never been late for class."

Have two representatives from Team A stand up. Student 1 reads the quoted speech aloud, and Student 2 changes it to reported speech.

S1: Darla said, "I love doing homework on the weekend."
S2: She said she loved doing homework on the weekend.

If the reported speech is correct, the team gets a point. The team with the most points at the end of the game wins.

Fun with grammar

Unit 10, 5 Practice, page 91

For the teacher: Form two teams. Draw a tic-tac-toe grid on the board. Put the following words in the grid (one word in each box): strong, hungry, sad, thirsty, surprised, cold, beautiful, loud, tall. Next, give each team a list with the following strong adjectives: gorgeous, furious, towering, starving, powerful, shocked, parched, miserable, deafening, freezing. Quickly go over the list with the students, helping them identify the synonyms (strong-powerful, hungry-starving, etc.). Then have a representative from Team A try to get a box for his or her team by saying two sentences that use the synonyms. For example, *The lion is a very strong animal. The lion is a powerful animal.* The student, if correct, can then put an X or an O in the box that has the word *strong* in it. The game continues until one team gets three boxes in a row.

Unit 11, 11 Practice, page 102

For the teacher: Write the following sentence on the board:

> The kids were asked to leave their shoes outside so the rug would stay clean.

Ask the class to tell you the *wh-* questions that would elicit this sentence.

What: What were the kids asked to do? (they were asked to leave their shoes outside)

Where: Where were the kids asked to leave their shoes? (outside)

Why: Why were the kids asked to leave their shoes outside? (so the rug would stay clean)

Who: Who was asked to leave their shoes outside? (the kids)

Divide the class into teams and write a new sentence on the board. For example:

> The girl was given milk every day so she would have strong bones.

Each team must write *who, what, when,* and *why* questions to go with the sentence. The first team to finish writing all the questions correctly is the winner.

Unit 12, 12 Practice, page 113

For the teacher: Divide the class into two teams. Write unfinished sentences with subordinating conjunctions on slips of paper and put them in a box. You may use the following sentences or make up your own.

- She looks happy in spite of _____.
- We won the game even though _____.
- Although they don't like each other, _____.
- Antonio was wearing a T-shirt and shorts in spite of _____.
- He never writes or calls me. However, _____.
- James was voted Most Likely to Succeed in spite of _____.
- Even though I take my dog for a long walk every morning, _____.
- My parents have full-time jobs. However, _____.

Representatives from each team take turns drawing slips of paper. Each team works together to complete the unfinished sentences on their slips of paper. The completed sentences can be funny or serious. Every time a team makes up a grammatically correct sentence, it gets a point. The team with the most points wins.

Fun with grammar

Peer editing checklist

☐ **Is the vocabulary correct?**

This is very *danger*. → This is very **dangerous**.

☐ **Is the spelling correct?**

I thought you were an *acter*. → I thought you were an **actor**.

☐ **Do sentences and questions have the correct word order?**

She *should have not* said anything. → She **should not have** said anything.

☐ **Is the grammar correct?**

Kelly is in San Diego *help* her aunt. → Kelly is in San Diego **to help** her aunt.

Have you ever *rode* a trolley car? → Have you ever **ridden** a trolley car?

☐ **Are the paragraphs well organized and easy to understand?**

When I need advice, I talk to my friends. My mom and dad give me advice, too. My friends' advice is usually good. Sometimes it isn't good.

I talk to my friends **when** I need advice. **Their** advice is usually good, **but** sometimes it isn't. My mom and dad give me advice, too.

☐ **Is the main idea of each paragraph stated clearly? Do other sentences support the main idea? Is your train of thought clear? Are there any tangents?**

Education has to change in order to keep up with new inventions. Now students use computers. I have a computer at home, too. I learned how to use the computer when I was in kindergarten. My teachers sometimes use DVDs, TVs, and VCRs to teach us, plus they do a lot more with computers.

→ Education has to change in order to keep up with new inventions. **In the past, students used typewriters.** Now **they** use computers. **Other kinds of technology affect education, as well. For example,** my teachers sometimes use DVDs, TVs, and VCRs to teach us, **and they have a lot of educational software.**

☐ **Is the writing interesting? Does the writer use a style that makes you want to read what he or she has written?**

I'm getting ready for a big exam on Friday. That's why I'm studying in the library today, even though it's a Saturday. I want to do well on the exam.

→ Do you wonder what I'm doing here in the library on a Saturday? Shouldn't I be out playing soccer with my friends? It's not a mystery; it's exam week! I need to do well on Friday's exam.

134 Peer editing checklist

Word list

Let's get started.

actor, 3
baker, 2
beautiful, 2
boring, 2
clean the room, 3
clear the table, 3
comfortable –
   uncomfortable, 2
conductor, 3
cook lunch (or dinner), 3
dirty, 2
do the grocery
   shopping, 3
do the laundry, 2
doctor, 3
driver, 3
heavy, 2
history, 2
interesting, 2
iron the clothes, 3
languages, 2
light, 2
literature, 2
make the bed, 3
math, 2
music, 2
noisy, 2
patient – impatient, 2
physical education
   (P.E.), 2
pleasant – unpleasant, 2
poor, 2
professional –
   unprofessional, 2
quiet, 2
rich, 2
sailor, 3
science, 2
singer, 3
teacher, 3
ugly, 2
vacuum the floor, 3
wash the dishes, 3

Unit 1

act – actor, 9
bake – baker, 9
build – builder, 9
drive – driver, 9
drum – drummer, 9
edit – editor, 9
inn, 8
move, 6
notice, 13
run – runner, 9
sing – singer, 9
surf – surfer, 9
technology, 6
wait, 8
write – writer, 9

Unit 2

bike, 15
boat, 15
bus, 15
car, 15
ferry, 15
helicopter, 15
motorcycle, 15
plane, 15
real, 14
reason, 14
ship, 15
show up, 14
taxi, 15
tourist, 20
train, 15
truck, 15
well-known, 20

Unit 3

advice, 26
cancel, 24
cover for someone, 24
get along with
   someone, 25
get away with
   something, 25
get back to, 25
get over something, 25
get through
   something, 25
get to someone, 25
get together with
   someone, 25

Unit 4

behavior, 35
chopsticks, 39
confident –
   confidence, 35
custom, 39
difficult – difficulty, 35
excuse, 35
generous – generosity, 35
guests, 34
honest – honesty, 35
humble – humility, 35
jealous – jealousy, 35
kind – kindness, 35
nervous –
   nervousness, 35
patient – patience, 35
polite – politeness, 35
popular – popularity, 35
rude, 35
scold, 35
service, 35
silent – silence, 35
so far, 37
upset, 35

Unit 5

alcohol, 47
blame, 42
care – careful, 48
care – careless, 48
conclusion, 47
courage – courageous, 48
danger – dangerous, 48
distance, 47
impatience –
   impatient, 48
independence –
   independent, 48
jealousy – jealous, 48
overtake, 47
risk, 47
speed, 47
vehicle, 47
weakness – weak, 48

Unit 6

announcement, 57
close, 55
delete, 55
download, 55
drag, 55
gadget, 57
log off, 55
log on, 55
open, 55
persuasive, 57
prediction, 57
resolution, 57
save, 55
search the Internet, 55
specialize, 57
surf the Internet, 55
take off, 54

Word list

Unit 7
criticize, 68
go against, 63
go along with, 63
go back on, 63
go for, 63
go on, 63
go out, 63
go out with, 63
go over, 63
native, 68
reaction, 63

Unit 8
accomplish, 76
amaze – amazement, 72
atom bomb, 76
atoms, 76
concerned with, 76
destroy, 76
development, 76
doctorate, 76
excite – excitement, 72
frighten – fright, 72
genius, 76
interest – interest, 72
lovable, 76
photoelectric effect, 76
regret, 76
relativity, 76
shock – shock, 72
surprise – surprise, 72
theory, 76
thrill – thrill, 72

Unit 9
annoyed with, 80
break one's word, 81
complicated, 86
dread, 86
emotionally, 86
endless, 86
event, 86
give someone a break, 81
hectic, 86
identities, 86
keep one's fingers crossed, 81
look forward to, 81
make up one's mind, 81
play it by ear, 81
preplanned, 86
reconnect, 86
reunion, 80
scrutiny, 86

show off, 86
stressful, 86

Unit 10
according to, 91
confident, 91
devastated, 91
ecstatic, 91
exhausted, 91
fantastic, 91
huge, 91
natural wonders, 96
terrible, 91
terrified, 91
tiny, 91
volcano, 96
waterfall, 96

Unit 11
beach, 103
biodiversity, 98
carbon emission, 98
cliff, 103
climate, 98
coast, 103
coral reef, 99
deforestation, 98
desert, 103
drought, 98
face, 99
forest, 103
global warming, 99
growth, 98
hill, 103
hole, 98
lake, 103
mountain, 103
ozone layer, 98
population, 98
remain, 98
sea/ocean, 103
shrink, 98
solution, 98
supplies, 98
thinning, 98
threatened, 98
tight, 98
unsolved, 99
volunteer, 101

Unit 12
achieve, 114
ambitious, 111
arrogant, 111
bossy, 111

civil rights, 114
creative, 111
dependable, 111
extraordinary, 114
frustrated, 114
good-natured, 111
human dignity, 114
lecture, 114
lips, 114
loyal, 111
manage to, 114
meaning, 114
outgoing, 111
remind, 109
sensitive, 111
understanding, 111

Answers to Quizzes

Unit 2, page 20, Exercise 16
Answers:
1. San Francisco
2. San Diego
3. Napa Valley
4. Universal Studios
5. Los Angeles

Unit 4, page 40, Exercise 17
Answers:
1. You should have opened your present in front of your hosts. Don't put a present away without opening it. Your hosts might think that you don't like it. Once you've opened the present, you should thank them and show them that you really liked it.
2. No, you shouldn't have. Among Koreans and most Asians, it is considered polite to deny a compliment. Accepting it means a lack of humility.
3. No, you shouldn't have. You should have eaten with your fingers. In Morocco, eating with the hands is customary. You should wash your hands before the meal, but don't lick your fingers! Licking your fingers during a meal is definitely impolite, as it is in the United States.
4. No, you shouldn't have. Your friend may feel he or she has to give you the doll. In Russia, if a guest compliments an object, the host may feel obligated to give it to him or her.